The Politically Correct Totalitarian Indoctrination Camp of 1984 Exposed

The Politically Correct Totalitarian Indoctrination Camp of 1984 Exposed

Lucien Bracquemont

The Politically Correct Totalitarian Indoctrination Camp of 1984 Exposed

Copyright © 2024 by Lucien Bracquemont. All rights reserved.

No part of this publication may be reproduced, distributed, or transmitted in any form or by any means, including photocopying, recording, or other electronic or mechanical methods, without the prior written permission of the author, except in the case of brief quotations embodied in critical reviews and certain other noncommercial uses permitted by copyright law.

The contents of this work, including, but not limited to, the accuracy of events, people, and places depicted; opinions expressed; permission to use previously published materials included; and any advice given or actions advocated are solely the responsibility of the author, who assumes all liability for said work and indemnifies the publisher against any claims stemming from publication of the work.

Printed in the United States of America
ISBN 978-1-64133-824-0 (sc)
ISBN 978-1-64133-919-3 (e)

2024.07.23

This book is printed on acid-free paper.

Because of the dynamic nature of the Internet, any web addresses or links contained in this book may have changed since publication and may no longer be valid. The views expressed in this work are solely those of the author and do not necessarily reflect the views of the publisher, and the publisher hereby disclaims any responsibility for them.

Blue Ink Media Solutions
1111B S Governors Ave
STE 7582 Dover,
DE 19904

www.blueinkmediasolutions.com

"We are faced with the paradoxical fact that education has become one of the chief obstacles to intelligence and freedom of thought."

-Bertrand Russell,
British philosopher (1872-1970)

Russell was correct. My experience in the 1980's shows the frightening truth of Russell's wisdom.

It is helpful to describe what this work is, and what it is not, along with my reasons for writing it.

It is highly painful to be aware of the very deep divisions in the United States of America, and elsewhere as well, the tremendous political and other divisions, the rapid deterioration of our economy, along with other threats to national and international well-being. The need is truly great to examine the need for a true analysis of the proper meaning of social justice and equality for all. This work is an analysis of the highly divisive nature of a movement that loudly proclaims to represent "equality for all," but is instead highly classist, highly authoritarian, and which gets its influence and power from simplistic fallacies, intimidation, censorship, demonizing any opposition or challenges to its rigid dogmas and its black-and-white-and-no-gray absolutism and stereotyping. I'm referring to POLITICAL CORRECTNESS.

This work, however, is in no way advocating "right-wing" ideologies or solutions. That is what it is NOT. It instead promotes a new, far more inclusive paradigm for equality and social justice than the ideologies of either the right or the left.

While I am blessed with a spiritual home, that is my church, I currently have no political home. From 1981 to 1985 I became strongly influenced by the Christian Right. This started in 1981, when Marion Pat Robertson convinced me that the American Civil Liberties Union was a relentless, bigoted, intolerant opponent of religious freedom. I'm not trying to convince anyone to change their opinion of the ACLU in either direction, I'm mentioning this for its historical significance, and because one of the major causes of the Christian Right to rise was the sincere belief of many Christians that the ACLU was a threat to religious freedom, in addition to the growing opposition of Evangelicals to abortion. The view that the Republican Party was far more protective of religious freedom and opposed to abortion caused millions of Christians, most of whom were formerly Democrats, to change their allegiance. This opposition to the Democrats/liberals/leftists was increased and strengthened by reaction to the rise of rigidly enforced Political Correctness in academia and other institutions.

Though I was a registered Democrat until 1984, then became an Independent, and was never registered as a Republican, I became strongly inclined to vote Republican. My strong leaning toward the "GOP" suddenly shattered in January of 2021, with the Insurrection on January 6, with the result that, in my opinion, both parties have become little more than useless, divisive, and toxic. I will clearly assert that Political Correctness contributed to this division and strife, and that Political Correctness was by nature highly divisive and will later explain why. Though this material is highly critical of Political Correctness, it is by no means a treatise for anything "right-wing." I feel that both the left-wing and right-wing have failed miserably. I invite my readers to approach this work with an open mind and to withhold judgment till they have read it extensively. I give the Republicans credit for protecting and strengthening religious freedom, and a couple of other issues, but not for much else. I feel strongly that the true needs of the large majority of the population are not being met by either party. I regard Political Correctness in general, and Radical Feminism (the very heart of Political Correctness for many years) in particular, to be highly classist despite their loud claims to be the ultimate in "equality." I do not expect anyone to accept this opinion without explanation or reasons for this, and I will provide many reasons for my view. By "classist", I mean that Political Correctness and Radical Feminism favor the wealthy and their interests over the poor and working class and middle class. These ideologies, despite their loud and highly debatable claims, do not represent "equality for all," or even most women.

Now on with the main body of this work.

I graduated from college in late 1984. There was a shift at that college very suddenly at that time. College changed from education to indoctrination.

At this time, an ideology foisted upon academia by a self-serving, greedy, power-hungry ELITE successfully subverted the meaning of justice, especially social justice, and equality to intimidate and censor any intellectual development, critical analytical thinking, and freedom of thought, well beyond anything that Bertrand Russell could have predicted. This subversion, though nobody realized it at the time, was classist in the extreme degree, and therefore anything but egalitarian. It suppressed and prevented the development of intellectual skills desperately needed for progress. It pretended to be the ultimate movement for "equality," and to champion the rights of the "oppressed." In reality, it was a front to promote the selfish interests of an elite composed overwhelmingly by white male multi-millionaires and billionaires. It not only deceived millions, but intimidated any challenges and dissent. It convinced millions that it labeled as "oppressed" into thinking that it served their needs, rights, and interests while it was merely employing the strategy of "divide and conquer" and used the "oppressed" as tools to serve its own interests.

The Politically Correct Totalitarian Indoctrination Camp of 1984 Exposed

The ideology to which I am referring is POLITICAL CORRECTNESS. I believe that PC was forced upon academia by a secret, hidden, ultra-powerful ELITE which cared not one bit about those who were truly oppressed. Why do I believe that this elite existed? Because PC became so rigidly enforced in academia in such a short period of time and with such intensity, and as I shall document, the rigidly enforced dogmas of PC served the interests of the Elite. I do not believe that college professors were so totally devoid of diversity of viewpoint and critical analytical skills that they could have all decided at once that the fallacies and simplistic analyses of PC were correct. ONLY a highly powerful ELITE could have accomplished this in such a short period of time. Undoubtedly many college professors were not convinced by PC ideology, but those that weren't convinced were highly and immediately intimidated by PC and quickly learned that their careers and livelihood depended on conformity to PC. This was a tremendous defeat to the potential of intellectuals and social progress and freedom of thought. I feel intensely that intellectuals and intellectual freedom are highly necessary for social progress, but the PC enforcers vehemently thought that they had all the answers, as simplistic and fallacious as PC ideology was. PC was totalitarian. The capture of academia was a tremendous victory for the totalitarian elitists of PC. It destroyed by intimidation and censorship the intellectual freedom needed for progress, and PC gets its extreme power almost exclusively by intimidation and censorship. It also misled millions into believing that PC was supported by the finest of "intellectuals," while in reality PC is pseudo-intellectual and very dangerously anti-intellectual by turning education into indoctrination, and PC made it virtually impossible for people to get ahead in society by making it very difficult to gain entrance into most influential fields without having to pass through several years of PC indoctrination, intimidation, and censorship.

Nor did the control and power of the PC elite end with the capture of academia. Before much longer the PC elite gained control of the news media, Hollywood, the liberally-oriented "mainline" churches, and other major cultural institutions.

From 1985 to 1987, I attended a seminary for training to be ordained as a clergyman. I was not there long before I detected that the seminary was rigidly controlled by PC enforcers. Constant intimidation was there daily. Not all students, of course, were convinced by PC, but we all knew that we had to conform, or keep our feelings to ourselves, or we knew that our careers would be destroyed. PC obsessions, dogmas and priorities were equated with the "Kingdom of God," and regarded as "prophetic."" No one dared challenged the simplistic and easily disputable dogmas of PC.

Many of the dogmas and pretensions of PC actually are distortions of views which gained currency in the 1960's, many of which were totally valid. Such views included the civil rights movement, which quite properly taught that people should be judged as individuals and not by group membership and to reject stereotypes, and that women should have equal pay for equal work. These views were morally legitimate and had great potential for improving the world. PC zealots, however, perverted and corrupted these noble views. While many of the doctrines, values, and attitudes of PC originated long before 1984, it was in 1984 that PC made the PC distortions mandatory and enforced, and it was then that all dissent from them was no longer tolerated.

The "women's lib(eration)" movement exploded into prominence in the late 1960's, and was a mixed bag. The view that women should have equal pay for equal work was totally legitimate (though Feminists would later demand, at least implicitly, equal pay for Unequal work), but women's libbers attacked the institutions of family and marriage, and were widely criticized for their anti-family views. They attacked family and marriage as "created by male chauvinists to keep women stuck with children and to prevent them from reaching their full potential." I can agree with women's libbers that not all women need to get married and have children and should have a wider variety of choices than offered to them before the 1970's, but the premise that the only way that women could have "fulfillment" and that all or most women could have the upscale careers that Feminists consider desirable was a serious fallacy that is quite easily repudiated, and of which hardly anyone is aware. I've done my research, and documented that only about 3% (three percent) of MEN have the upscale careers that Feminists consider so necessary for "fulfillment." Only about three percent of MEN are "doctors, lawyers," engineers, executives, etc.(1) If women were guaranteed half of these careers, only about three percent of women would have them. I acknowledge that women should be allowed to enter these careers on an INDIVIDUAL equal opportunity basis, with no preferential treatment (affirmative action or quotas) and no discrimination against men. If a woman wants to be an engineer, fine. But if a top-notch engineering school requires a 3.3 undergraduate average for a "white male" to be admitted, the same should apply to a female applicant. This what equality means in this instance, and Feminists (and PC enforcers) do NOT want equality in this instance; they want preferential treatment for women. The statistical fact that only three percent of men have such careers, if it became widely known, would be fatal to much Feminist and PC propaganda.

One problem not widely noticed, is that Feminism, at least after it became infected by PC, is highly, highly CLASSIST and that for that reason is not the "ultimate" in equality that it so loudly proclaims to be. This would make Feminism highly useful to the "white male" multi-millionaires and billionaires that would later incorporate radical Feminism into their PC ideology. The classism of radical Feminism would also be useful to the PC elite for other reasons, which I shall later address. There are many reasons why Feminism is highly classist. Feminists widely oppose recognition for women in traditional female roles. They widely denounce support for women in traditional roles as a form of "patriarchal oppression" to keep women out of the upscale careers that Feminists so strongly emphasize. This is not only a fallacy, as only three percent of women would have such careers if women were guaranteed half of them, but it is a form of CLASS DISCRIMINATION. Feminism is NOT perfect equality, no matter what Feminists claim or what people naively believe. When faced with the reality that not all women hold Feminist upper-middle-class and upper-class values, Feminists and PC enforcers typically respond that such women are indoctrinated by the "oppressive patriarchy." Some Feminists have even claimed that women have no natural desire for family and children; they have such desires only because the "patriarchy" has indoctrinated them into having such views. All these Feminist views are classist and fallacious. It is also my view that one reason why the PC Elite incorporated radical Feminism into the very heart of PC ideology was because most of this elite was strongly influenced by anti-family values due to their view that the world was over-populated and that population growth was undesirable. The anti-family features of Feminism made it highly useful to the PC elite.

The weakening of the family structure, and absence of fathers in the home, and abandonment of children by their fathers, have hurt "women and minorities" far more than they have hurt "white males." It has become increasingly obvious to many that weak family structures have hurt millions and especially children from minority communities. While I am not to place all the blame for this upon radical Feminism and rigid enforcement of PC dogmas, I feel that they deserve very much of the blame. If, as Feminists claim, "patriarchy" is such an evil and "oppressive" influence, then children would be better off without fathers. Any deadbeat dad could argue, "Since 'patriarchy' is so evil and oppressive, I'll spare my children from it. I'll leave my girlfriend to raise our children alone. She can 'reach her full potential' better without me in her home." Such a reprehensible and hideous abandonment of responsibility is a logical outcome of PC/Feminist ideology.

Another big reason why the PC elite used Feminism and issues of racism to its advantage was because of the well-known strategy of "divide and conquer." PC zealots became OBSESSED with promoting the highly divisive stereotypes that all "white males" are "oppressors," while everyone else was "oppressed." This PERVERTED the highly moral view of civil rights activists that all stereotypes are wrong and unjust, and that people should be judged as individuals rather than by group membership. Institutions controlled by the PC elite soon began to promote this modified form of class warfare, and constantly promoted the stereotypes that women were "oppressed" and that men were "oppressors." This was widely promoted in the mid-to-late 1980's to an extreme degree in the news media, academia, and the "mainline" churches, and there was intense intimidation and censorship of anyone who dared object. This form of class warfare was enhanced by affirmative action, which predated PC but was used by PC effectively to promote the PC/Feminist obsession with how everyone else was "oppressed" by "white males," to demonize "white males" as people who did not deserve to be protected from discrimination, and to promote their power-hungry goal of conquering by dividing. Most PC enforcers and Feminists feel that discrimination against men, especially "white males," should not be considered discrimination. And indoctrinating women and certain minorities into believing that all "white males" are their oppressors promoted hatred, bitterness, and resentment, useful for the PC strategy of "divide and conquer." It was also highly useful to the PC elite by placing the blame and condemnation upon "white males" collectively, rather than blaming the top 1% who have most of the power. This also represented gross hypocrisy on the part of the PC elite. If there was ever an "oppressive patriarchy" it was the PC elite. One barely known reason for the "gender wage gap" hoax is that the top 1% of men earn or possess 20-40% of male income,(2) which greatly skews upward the "average" male income. PC/Feminism condemn men collectively for the "gender wage gap" rather than singling out the small elite. Thus, all men, not just those at the top, are condemned and demonized. If the PC elite, composed overwhelmingly by greedy white male plutocrats, were really concerned about "equality" then it would voluntarily redistribute its income to those less wealthy. In addition, these elitists would volunteer to practice affirmative action against themselves, and resign their wealthy, powerful positions to increase "diversity" and weaken "patriarchy." This is another documentation of how PC ideology benefits the PC elite.

In the 1990's I read a book, now discarded, which vividly illustrates the highly classist nature of PC/Feminism. The author was a male doctor who, though strongly influenced by Feminism, was generally pro-life and had never performed an abortion, though he was cynical of "The pro-life movement... [as] an attempt to give women whose work involves the home the same prestige and status as career women." (3) These pro-life activists were actually promoting equality, whereas their Feminist/PC critics were promoting classism or class discrimination. So much for the highly naïve foolishness that

Feminism is a victory "for all humankind," not even for all or even most women.

Hardly anyone realizes this, but the PC/Feminist demand for upper-class gender quotas benefits the richest 1% of "white males" more than they benefit 99% of women, while protecting the wealth, power, and privilege of the rich. They, along with other concepts of PC, orient our culture toward the fallacy that "equality" and "social justice" can co-exist with a heavy concentration of wealth in the top 1%, multi-millionaires and billionaires, while neglecting the poor, the working class, and the middle class, along with the PC dogma that "racism (which indeed is evil) and sexism," which dogma has been rigidly promoted by PC since 1984, as the greatest evils in our society. Racism is indeed highly evil, but PC will not solve this problem. The dogma that racism and sexism are the greatest evils is simplistic and ignores the reality that CLASSISM and the GREED of the wealthy cause, which "disproportionately affect" minorities, but this dogma protects the wealth and privilege of the wealthy plutocrats. I feel strongly that a big reason why efforts to eliminate RACISM have not been more successful is because of the failure to attach racism to CLASSISM, which hurts minorities more than "white males." But then, attacking classism and greed will threaten the wealthy plutocrats. In addition, classism and greed affect the vast majority, including even most "white males." And, if most people realized this, then the PC elite would be less effective in pitting everyone else against "white males" which would hamper the PC elite's strategy of "divide and conquer."

Despite the simplistic fallacy that "racism and sexism" are the greatest causes of evil while being silent about classism and greed, charges of "racism and sexism" have been a highly powerful method of censoring and intimidating any dissent from PC. Anytime anyone in an institution controlled by PC enforcers, who expressed and objection to the rigid dogmas of PC, will be quickly intimidated and censored by accusations of "racism and sexism," no matter how unjust the accusations may be.

Perhaps the greatest tool of intimidation and censorship by PC since 1984 has been PC's demand for the absolute censorship of so-called "sexist language." Without this censorship and demand for total compliance, those who were not convinced by the simplistic, authoritarian dogmas of PC could keep silent and keep their dissent to themselves, but the censorship of "sexist language" meant that such neutrality was no longer possible. Those who were unconvinced by PC were forced to comply, and the PC rigid enforcement of PC speech codes was a constant reminder that the PC zealots were always on the guard to intimidate any dissent. At my seminary, this was an extreme method of intimidation. It frequently occurred that some professor would utter some PC propaganda, but many times a day people were forced to change words in the prayers or liturgy, and anytime that anyone opened their mouths, the PC speech police were there to intimidate and demand total compliance. It was not possible to avoid PC intimidation on an hourly basis.

I once read an interesting article by a male, mainline Protestant minister, expressing the view that many of his fellow clergy felt trapped in an alien hostile system, counting down the days to their retirement. I can understand his feelings. These clergy knew that conformity to PC dogmas was necessary for their livelihood, and that their livelihoods would be destroyed if they stepped out of line. So much for the naïve idea that PC equals justice and liberation! It really represents oppression.

I once knew a co-worker who formerly worked as a janitor at a local rigidly PC university. One would expect that, as a janitor rather than a professor or student, his exposure to PC would have been minimal, but he complained that it was everywhere, unavoidable, and in everyone's face, and highly annoying.

There are undoubtedly hundreds of college professors, mainline clergy, journalists, etc. who correctly detect the fallacies and other deficiencies of PC ideology, but know that their livelihoods depend on conformity and are thus effectively silenced, an unfortunate reminder that true education hardly exists now and had been replaced with a totalitarian form of indoctrination camps, which effectively prevent freedom of thought and true intellectual development. Because of PC, we have lost nearly 40 years in the struggle for progress, true social justice, and true equality.

It has long struck me as strange and incongruous that so many educated, economically secure women are more likely to see themselves and all women as "oppressed" and are highly bitter about it, while less educated, working-class women are far less bitter about life. This can be easily explained: to enter most decent-paying occupations, one must attend college for several years. In colleges since 1984, a student is DAILY indoctrinated with anti-male, classist PC propaganda, indoctrinated into the falsehood that PC equals "equality for all," and subjected to PC censorship and PC intimidation. It is nothing short of totalitarian that people need to be subjected to such in order to receive an education enabling them to gain a decent standard of living.

An excellent example of the true nature of PC is the following: In recent years it has become increasingly common to state that the weakened family structures that prevail in minority communities have greatly hurt these minorities, especially their children. Even some liberally-minded people have begun to express such feelings. Yet, from 1984 to 2022, anyone who dared express such a view would have been demonized by PC enforcers as "racist and sexist." Thus, due to PC intimidation and censorship, decades have been lost that could have been used to strengthen minority households, and greatly benefited minorities. So much for the argument that PC represents the welfare and dignity of minorities! PC masquerades as the ultimate in "equality" and the PC enforcers loudly claim to be the protectors and saviors of the "oppressed" and of "women and minorities" but the FACTS loudly indicate otherwise. Additionally, the weakening of the family has hurt women more than it has hurt "white males." If it is no longer possible to support a family on one income, will it be easier for unmarried and divorced mothers to do so?

According to PC dogma, the ideal for "equality" is this: if women had the exact per capita of income as men, and were guaranteed at least half of all upper-class careers, and millionaires' and billionaires' positions, and "white males" were "proportionately" represented among the poorest and disadvantaged, this would mean "full equality," would benefit all women, and possibly a utopia and a victory for "all humankind." It would do LITTLE at all to promote equality for anyone. It would not promote equality for many in the bottom 95% or so, including women, and it would promote extreme privilege for those in the top 1%. The "women earn 76 cents" statistic, widely promoted in the news media and other institutions controlled by the PC elite, is a highly misleading statistic, and based on a simplistic, invalid method. I INTENSELY and unreservedly support equal pay for EQUAL work, but this is not sufficient for the PC zealots or the Feminists that they manipulate. It ignores the fact that women work an average of 7% (seven percent) fewer hours per capita than men,(4) that the top 1% of men possess 20-40% of male income and wealth (which skews upward the average male per capita income), and is not even based on comparing men and women in the same occupation. Ironically, anti-male affirmative action has also contributed to this "gap." Because of anti-male AA on college campuses, and the profoundly anti-male atmosphere in academia, in many occupations women earn less than men because they often are younger than their male counterparts, and therefore have less experience. The "76 cents" statistic has been extremely powerful in promoting the PC agenda. It is nothing less than a hoax, but that does not deter the PC enforcers or their Feminist puppets. All they care or know about is that it WORKS. It is highly powerful. And the widespread promotion of the "76 cent" hoax by the news media, the "mainline" churches, and academia is very strong evidence that these institutions are controlled by the PC Elite.

One reason why I have been highly critical of Feminism (or more accurately the PC Elite that has gained control over the Feminists and manipulated them for their own greedy, elitist, and totalitarian aims) is that Feminism defines "equality" exclusively in gender terms, (and since the mid-1980's usually in collective gender terms), with no concern for equality for the poor, the working class, or the middle class. I believe intensely, and unreservedly, that women and men of all races are equally the Image of God and have a right to a decent, equitable, and sufficient standard of living, that there is biblical support for this view, and will promote EQUALITY for most, including most women. I shall get to this later. However, by defining "equality" in a way that benefits the rich and accommodates and protects their greed, PC/Feminism is highly CLASSIST, opposed to the welfare and needs of the less wealthy, and is at best highly INADEQUATE as a basis of equality.

It must be noted that any reference to the existence of PC and the PC Elite before 1991 is somewhat of an anachronism, which greatly increased the power of the PC Elite. I never heard the terms "political correctness" or "politically correct" until 1991, though I immediately knew that the powerful force that they represented dated back to 1984. This would greatly strengthen the power of the PC Elite. Since PC had no name for the first seven years of its existence, it was much harder to identify, label, or even detect. It made it impossible to detect the existence of the PC Elite itself by making this elite hidden and invisible. The existence of the Freemasons, the world's largest secret society, is widely known. Far less widely known is the existence of the Trilateralists and Bilderbergers, and these exclusive, powerful elite secret societies would be hardly known at all if it were not for "conspiracy theorists" who expose their existence. I am not endorsing the conspiracy theorists or their views. The power of secret societies comes largely from their secrecy, their hiddenness, and the largely public unawareness of them or their secret doctrine. The PC Elite learned how the secret societies gain control by remaining hidden, hard to detect, and keeping their secrecy. The PC Elite knew this well. For seven years they made their existence undetectable. And, many years after 1991, still very few people have detected it. The PC Elite, unlike the Freemasons, made their doctrines well known, but the truly fallacious, greedy, elitist, and extremely classist nature of their dogmas remains hidden. Those who have detected their true nature are easily intimidated and censored, and millions still believe that PC represents equality and justice for "all."

While the PC enforcers loudly proclaim the dogmas of PC, there are many SECRETS of PC that are barely known, most of which I detected on my own and have exposed. Among these secrets: PC is a highly authoritarian, even totalitarian ideology, that far from being a progressive movement for social justice and equality, it is extremely classist and elitist, that it is a tremendous obstacle to social justice and equality by preventing true intellectual development and freedom of thought, that it gets its power from censorship and intimidation, that its concepts of "equality" are anything but that, among others. These are what PC truly represents, though very few people realize this.

WHY I WROTE THIS: My motives for this work are not fame and notoriety or monetary profit. My motives include a concern for true freedom, true social justice, and true equality for all, rather than the corruption of these concepts by PC. Endeavoring for true social justice and equality, under any conditions, is very long, arduous, and requires intellectual development, freedom of thought, open discussion, and DIVERSITY OF OPINIONS and a clear understanding of what justice and equality for all really mean. The biggest obstacle at this time, and since 1984, is PC. The PC enforcers think that they have all the answers and unaware of their manipulation by the PC Elite who actually know the true nature of PC. Unfortunately, any discussions, dialogue, intellectual and philosophical reflection, and other necessary methods are impossible with PC. Anyone who challenges the rigid dogmas of PC, or even discussed their inadequacies and shortcomings, will immediately be taken as a threat by the PC enforcers, who will immediately demonize any challenge to PC dogmas as "racist and sexist."

In order to endeavor for true social justice, progress, and equality it will be necessary to expose the true nature of PC as the counterfeit of social justice and equality that it is, and this will require a tremendous amount of work and effort. It took me decades to develop this critique of the true nature of PC.

Nearly all "social justice" activists, whether secular, in the mainline churches, and even a few "Evangelicals" are almost totally influenced and manipulated by PC. They do not realize that they have been deceived.

While I dismiss the "progressive" activists in the mainline churches for their naivete, and many conservative Christians dismiss social justice as a front for Marxism, I have chosen a different path, one far more difficult. I think that there is a great need for an alternative approach to social justice and equality, one informed by biblical principles, without the toxicity and simplistic fallacies of PC.

PC was certainly correct in denouncing racism, though it condemned many people for racism that were innocent. Their use of the term "sexism," though, was overly broad and subject to abuse. It essentially meant anything different from PC views on gender. This view that racism and "sexism" were the exclusive causes of evil in America, though, was simplistic, and ironically protected the wealth of the most wealthy and privileged. I feel that classism and the greed of the wealthy and powerful were greater causes of evil, that classism and greed afflict minorities more than they afflict "white males," and that the efforts to eliminate racism will be ineffective without attacking classism. The PC solution to fighting "sexism" was to place an extreme emphasis on the interests and power of upper-class women while ignoring or downplaying the values of other women, and to promote policies and attitudes that benefit upper-class women more than anyone else, while demonizing as "sexist" any efforts to argue that such an approach benefits upper-class women more than anyone else. PC insisted that upper-class gender quotas were necessary for "full, perfect and complete equality," though they did nothing to benefit those, including women, of lower income or social status. They redefined "equality" to mean anything that benefited upper-class women above everyone else, and demonized anyone as "sexist" who could detect the inadequacies of such an approach. Anyone could see the injustices of the claim that all men (including the poorest) were "oppressors" and that all women (including the wealthiest) were "oppressed," (if such an assertion were true then poverty would not exist among men), but anyone who dared challenge this blatant fallacy would be demonized as "sexist." The term "sexist" was used very powerfully as a method of intimidation and censorship. If someone reasoned that there were higher priorities than upper-class gender quotas, such a person would be afraid to express such an opinion due to charges of "sexism." Essentially, to the PC enforcers, the interests and power of upper-class women were the highest priority of all, and anyone who felt otherwise was condemned as "sexist." If a lower-income "white male" objected to being condemned as an "oppressor," he would be denounced as "sexist," as would anyone who felt that the needs of the poor and working class were more important.

PC had a very distorting effect on the concept of "social justice" in the "progressive" mainline churches. Previously social justice was understood as providing and advocating for the needs and dignity of the poor. That changed when PC gained control of the mainline churches. The term "poor" became replaced with the "oppressed," and suddenly these churches abandoned the needs and rights of the poor. Lower-income men were now condemned as "oppressors," and the preferential option for the poor became replaced with the preferential option for the rich, though very few people realized it at the time. Social justice was redefined as whatever promoted the interests of upper-middle-class and upper-class women, in the name of opposing "sexism" and "oppression."

I will state that I am in no way opposed to the entrance of women into upscale occupations. I have personally benefited from the services of several of them. But I do not consider an upscale woman who earns more than 97% of men to be "oppressed," and male taxicab drivers and low-paid laborers to be "oppressors." Nor do I believe that upper-class gender quotas represent full, complete, or perfect equality for all. I also feel that the extreme emphasis of PC upon racism and "sexism," while being silent about greed and classism, fails to address some real evils, and also fails to indict the top economic class for its extreme greed, while placing the blame on all "white males," rather than singling out the real culprits. This served the interests of the wealthiest.

There is need for diversity in the efforts toward social justice, and I do not mean diversity as the PC zealots define it, namely, men and women and LGBTQ's of all ethnicities and races enforcing the same PC simplistic crap. I mean people of diverse viewpoints, social and economic classes, levels of education, and occupations and faiths. Probably even some PC advocates should be included. However, PC zealots would feel that ONLY PC zealots should be included. In such a setting, there is NO room for PC indoctrination, PC censorship, or PC intimidation.

I want to make it clear that I repudiate all misogyny, and bear no cynicism or animosity to women as a whole, and repudiate any form of female collective guilt, as well as any other form of collective guilt. I now feel that even the Feminists are not the real problem; the real problem is the mostly male, hidden PC Elite that used and manipulated the Feminists for the PC Elite's evil agenda.

I once heard of a man whose mother was a Holocaust survivor. One cannot get much more oppressed than being a European

Jew who went through the Holocaust. Unfortunately, she molested her son several times. When she did this, she ceased to be oppressed and became an OPPRESSOR. But, according to PC dogma, she will always be oppressed simply because she is female, and the son will always be an oppressor simply because he is male. Her son confessed that he became highly misogynistic because of his mother's molestation of him, though he later overcame his placing of his mother's guilt onto other women. He did not become misogynistic because the "evil white males" or the "oppressive patriarchy" led him to do so. The mother was responsible for her son's misogyny, though this misogyny was not the proper or just response to his mother's criminal behavior, which the son later realized. Unfortunately, PC is useless for opposing collective guilt, since it teaches that "white males" should be condemned collectively, and thus guides people toward practicing collective guilt. All forms of racism, anti-Semitism, and misogyny are based at least partly on collective guilt, and the Holocaust could not have happened without it. The failure of PC zealots to realize this shows how PC is a COUNTERFEIT of social justice and equality.

Now on to an alternative view. I feel that the Bible provides some very helpful texts to analyze social injustice, and to provide some very helpful principles for social justice, though they are nearly universally ignored or distorted.

Start with Genesis 1:27: "God created man (or "hu"man"kind") in his image. Male and female he made them." This text is widely quoted by Christians of nearly all varieties, though nearly all of them fail to realize its complete implications, or (mostly "progressives") distort and corrupt the true meaning. As "progressives" quickly assert, it supports gender equality. To be sure. But does not merely mean that; it means the equality of everyone. We must be very careful, and "progressives" fail at this, but it does not necessarily support equality as OUR SURROUNDING CULTURE, or as the news media, or politicians, define equality. "Progressives" would take the totally correct assertion that it teaches gender equality (so far so good) but then conclude that it supports Radical Feminism. One problem with this: a woman who earns 20 times the average per capita income, and of course a man who earns 20 times the average per capita income, are no more God's image than a taxicab driver, a truck driver, a waitress, or a nurse's aide. The wealthy have no more rights from being made in the image of God than anyone else. I am not a communist; there are legitimate reasons why, say, a highly educated, highly-skilled professional should earn several times more than many others. Not everyone is equal in skills, education, experience, the amount of years and money spent in acquiring an education, personal responsibility, as well as other variables. These justify some inequalities in income. However, while there are some legitimate reasons why some people earn several times more than others, being created in the image of God is not among them. The rich are no more God's image than the poor. Certainly, someone who borrowed millions of dollars to buy a burger franchise, with huge debts and great risks and responsibilities, should earn many times as much as a "burger flipper." And, when it comes to legitimate inequalities in income, justified by greater responsibilities, skills, risks, etc., enough is enough! It is totally justified for some people to earn 6 to 10 times the average per capita income. But to demand multi-million dollar salaries is not justified, and should be denounced as greed regardless of the gender of whoever practices greed. I will provide biblical support for this position.

One of the greatest stands against social injustice and inequality ever taken is Ephesians 5:5. "No greedy person, in effect an idolater, has any share in the Kingdom of Christ and of God." This explicitly states that greed is contrary to the Kingdom of God, yet not only have "progressive" mainline church activists failed to realize this; they even contradict it. When they say that it promotes God's Kingdom when certain people become greedy and fabulously wealthy, they are actually opposing God's Kingdom.

I shall now proceed to the finest assertion of social justice and equality ever written, 5 verses only, but it took a stronger stand for social justice and equality in these few verses than any Feminist or PC zealot took in a whole volume, "There is great gain in religion, provided that one is content with a sufficiency. We brought nothing into this world and we can take nothing out. If we have food and clothing we have all that we need. Those who aim to get rich are falling into a snare and a trap... Some have made shipwrecks of their souls. The love of money is the root of all evil." (1 Timothy 6:6-10)

Note: it does not say that no one should be allowed to have more than a sufficiency, merely that one should be content with such. It uses hyperbolic language. Obviously, we need more than food and clothing. We need housing, some level of education, transportation, insurance, and other things. The true meaning is to distinguish between needs and mere desires. We need housing, but we do not need mansions. We need transportation, but we don't need exclusive European luxury yuppie cars. Paul (or whatever the PEDANTIC higher critics want us to call the author) took a strong stand for true social justice and equality in this passage. It says that the love of money is the root of all evil. It does not say that "sexism" is the root of all evil. The evil nature of greed applies, regardless of the gender or nationality of those who practice it.

Placing these three texts together, we can make a powerful case for equality and social justice. Since everyone is equally the image of God, everyone has equal rights that proceed from that status. Greed is evil and contrary to God's Kingdom, regardless of who practices it. Greed never promotes God's Kingdom, no matter how much "intersectionality" someone might claim. The true meaning of social justice is a sufficiency for all. After these PRIORITIES have been addressed, then is the time to address issues such as upper-class gender quotas, the "glass ceiling," and other issues that benefit the rich above the poor. Unfortunately, PC zealots have their priorities upside-down.

When I think about the very serious issues facing the majority of Americans today, such as how 60% of us are living paycheck-to-paycheck, a majority of adults are only one bill for auto repairs or medical expenses away from bankruptcy, the once-dominant middle class is shrinking, millions of once securely middle-class families are falling into poverty, and I have even heard of doctors resorting to "pay day loans," yet according to PC, upper-class gender quotas will result in "equality for all."

It is indeed painful to see how our economy has failed and deteriorated during the last 3 decades. I am not saying that PC is directly responsible for most of this. But PC did not prevent it. Yet the rigidly enforced fallacies of PC at least indirectly contributed. Had the last 39 years been marked by open discussion, uninhibited debates, freedom of thought, and intellectual ferment, some of these blights could have been eased. PC's highly effective method of censorship, intimidation, and highly successful method of brainwashing prevented the intellectual development that could have yielded far more progress.

If a PC enforcer had said, "Feminism represents justice for all and is a victory for all humankind (and could likely lead to a utopia)," such an assertion would be asinine and silly in the extreme. But in an environment controlled by PC, the students who heard this simplistic opinion could react in any of the following four ways, 1) they may be naïve enough to believe it, 2) their intellectual potential would be stunted by PC so much that they would not realize its fallacious nature, 3) they would be so beleaguered and worn down by persistent PC propaganda that they have abandoned the will to resist and fight, or 4) they may detect the fallacious and invalid nature of the assertion, but they would not express their dissent because of PC censorship and intimidation; they knew that a vile accusation of "S!E!X!I!S!M!!!!" would result. This reveals the evil potential of PC. It served the purposes of one-sided propaganda and indoctrination. It reminded students that, no matter how illogical an assertion may be, it must be accepted with no debate, the same method used in Communist and Nazi indoctrination camps.

A major obstacle to social and economic progress today is the evil power of anti-intellectualism. By that I do not mean faithful Christians who do not believe in Darwinian evolution and higher criticism. I mean preventing and censoring the development of critical, analytical thinking, freedom of thought, freedom of inquiry, open-spirited debates, and other methods that produce true progress. These have been destroyed by PC totalitarian methods. One reason why the PC Elite targeted academia for its first takeover was because this elite realized that true intellectualism and freedom of thought were a big obstacle to the elite's plan to control the population. They realized the need to neutralize this obstacle. Now, in order to enter most influential occupations it is necessary to be subjected to PC indoctrination for several or more years. This is just as totalitarian as the methods of the Nazis or Communists. Also, as with the Nazis, the PC needed a "scapegoat" to be attacked. For the Nazis, this was the Jewish community collectively. The Nazis brainwashed the masses into believing that the Jewish community collectively was responsible for nearly all of Germany's problems. With the PC Elites, the scapegoat was "white males" collectively. And the PC zealots attempted to brainwash "women and minorities" to believe that "white males" collectively were responsible for their "oppression," and to demonize "white males" collectively and demand discrimination against them under the form of "affirmative action," and the claim that discrimination against "white males" should not be considered discrimination.

For many years, it was common for those who rejected PC to malign college professors as agents of evil, as they were supposedly the greatest propagators of PC. I feel that this is unjust. There was a minority of college professors who were decent and godly who did not believe in PC and found PC highly annoying. In a sense, college professors are among most oppressed groups of people in America today. In 1984, they lost their freedoms of thought, speech, inquiry, etc. when these freedoms were destroyed by PC. College professors probably have less freedom than nearly anyone else in America. Undoubtedly, a motive for many to become professors was to help others develop their intellectual potential, train people on how to think for themselves, challenge others to hear all sides of an issue, engage in open debates, and detect logical fallacies. These noble desires, so necessary for human progress, were quickly destroyed by that totalitarian ideology known as PC. Undoubtedly many potential professors entered college motivated by these truly intellectual methods, but after a few semesters of PC indoctrination and intimidation, they abandoned their aspirations.

Ironically, though I suffered through five semesters of PC enforcement, I could immediately see the fallacies, falsehoods, and the totalitarian nature of PC, PC actually helped me to develop my intellectual skills by bombarding me with fallacies and propaganda that I could easily debunk and dismiss. PC intimidation did not convince me of its dogmas, but it made my life very miserable.

Writing this has not been at all pleasant or enjoyable. It has placed much stress upon me, reminding me of unpleasant memories of the distant past. I regret that there is any need for this expose of PC. I regret that several others have not done so by now. Those who would have the intellectual potential to do so, or would have been qualified to do so, have had their potential abilities destroyed by PC, and those who would know well to expose effectively the evil character of PC have been threatened or intimidated. Totalitarian systems of the past, including Fascism, Nazism, Marxism, and Communism have been challenged and exposed by some highly courageous individuals who have been oppressed by them and could see the true nature of these evil systems, and who suffered imprisonment and even martyrdom. Then how come hardly anyone OPPRESSED by PC has had the courage to challenge and expose PC? Perhaps PC has been far more subtle and more successful at the arts of intimidation and deception. That is truly frightening to anyone concerned for freedom. It is especially frightening that in the United States of America, which supposedly is so uniquely great in its guarantees and supports for freedom, such a totalitarian force as PC could have originated. It is likely because the PC Elite realized that FREEDOM was their biggest obstacle to their plan of total power, and correctly realized that freedom had to be eliminated for their totalitarian plans to succeed.

This elite MAY be aiming for total world power and control. Since the 1970's many conspiracy theorists have been claiming that two highly powerful, international elite secret societies, the Trilateralists and the Bilderbergers, have been conspiring to set up a "one-world socialist government" that they would rigidly control. These two secret societies do indeed exist, and I have found their websites. I am not endorsing these conspiracy theories, and I do not know of any connection between them and the PC Elite, but I do believe that some PC Elite definitely exists, and that they are merciless in their lust for power.

It is highly disappointing to realize how the potential for true social justice and true equality was destroyed when the PC Elite gained control of the mainline churches in the mid-1980's. I shall illustrate: PC zealots and Radical Feminists would be likely to claim that it is necessary for "equality" that half of all the millionaires' and billionaires' positions must be guaranteed for women. Many "progressives" in these churches, totally unaware of the extreme CLASSISM in such an assertion, would respond by saying, "Since Genesis 1:27 says that God made male and female in his image, this proves this PC/Feminist claim." Does the Bible support equality? TO BE SURE. But such a simplistic, classist response shows a high degree of naivete and lack of rigorous intellectual analysis. Again, does the Bible support equality? TO BE SURE. But it is an extreme fallacy to assume that the Bible supports equality as OUR CULTURE, including the news media and academia define equality. Maybe the understanding of God and the Bible about equality differs from how our cultural milieu defines it. Maybe to God and the Bible equality does not mean that half the multi-millionaires' positions must be reserved for women. Maybe, instead, God and the Bible would have us believe that NO ONE should be a multi-millionaire, or at least until and unless everyone had a sufficiency. This illustrates the intense need for deep theological reflection, discussion, debating, seeking alternative views, and diversity of viewpoint, as distinguished from the simplistic views of PC. If I were allowed to participate in such a discussion, I would argue that the rich are no more God's image than anyone else, that the PC view of gender quotas is CLASSIST and does NOTHING to benefit the less wealthy (who are equal to millionaires as the images of God). Unfortunately, and tragically, such reflection and discussion are unlikely to occur in theological circles where PC enforcers are present. This is, to me, another example of the highly oppressive and totalitarian nature of PC. It also indicates the tremendous influence that PC has over the mainline churches.

I recently viewed a video of a young woman who felt that she was a happy young woman before she entered a private women's college, and how she became highly unhappy and angry as a result of the indoctrination that she received there, though she later de-programmed herself.(5) She was constantly indoctrinated into believing that an "oppressive patriarchy" controlled everything. There is SOME truth to that. An oppressive patriarchy does control academia. That oppressive patriarchy is the PC Elite. This also is an indication of the methods used by PC propagandists. They purposely try to make people angry, including those from highly privileged backgrounds. There is a reason for this method. Angry people are far easier to manipulate. The PC zealots succeed in making vast numbers of people angry. They make women very angry by indoctrinating them with the propaganda that all women are oppressed by "white males" and the "patriarchy," and they make "white males" angry by demonizing them as the "oppressors" of everyone else. This not only makes people easier to manipulate, it also promotes the "divide and conquer" strategy of the evil PC Elite. I daresay, the results of this PC scheme have played a very large role in the extreme divisions in America that are a big threat to peace and public welfare. It is acknowledged by many people of many persuasions that our nation is very badly polarized and that our very existence as a nation is at stake. It happened by design, not by chance.

PC employs an abusive method that guarantees it a victory no matter what, which could be called "If you can't beat them, join them." It was highly annoying to hear the same PC fallacies rammed down our throats at the seminary. It bordered on psychological abuse. Though I was never convinced that these fallacies were true, I paid a high price emotionally, which later led to a deep depression and mental illness. This infliction of emotional pain, of course, represented a victory for PC. Others, even if they could detect a fallacy, simply went along. If I had chosen this path, and been convinced of their dogmas, it would have possibly prevented a mental illness, but my ability to see the true nature of PC, along with my critical analytical thinking skills, would not allow me to take that easy path. "Ignorance is bliss," for those who succumbed to PC.

There is nothing greedy about expecting equal pay for equal work, equal individual rights before the law, and equal individual opportunity. In the 1960's and early 1970's, equitable, just, and legitimate civil rights laws were passed by the governments at all levels. However, PC deserves NO CREDIT for any of this. It happened before the PC Elite forced itself upon many influential institutions in 1984. The PC Elite discovered how it could distort, corrupt, and pervert these legitimate concepts to promote its evil, elitist, greedy, and power-hungry agenda. The Feminists annoyed many with their anti-family doctrines, but they rarely or never claimed that Feminism is a "victory for all humankind," that it represented perfect justice and equality for all, or that it had utopian potential. These fallacies came after PC gained control.

In analyzing PC fallacies and highly manipulative dogmas, we need to ask questions (which is a true threat to the PC tyrants), and keep asking them. Why do so many of us think that it promotes equality when a certain person becomes a multi-millionaire? Basically, because our culture says so. Then, why does our culture promote the mentality that it promotes equality when a certain person becomes a multi-millionaire? Because academia, the news media, Hollywood, and other institutions say so, even many mainline church leaders say so. Then, why do these institutions promote such a fallacy? Because they are controlled by a very powerful upper-class which uses them to promote cultural ideas and policies and philosophies that protect their selfish, power-hungry, and greedy interests. Plus, it is a logical fallacy to believe that being a multi-millionaire promotes equality, regardless of the gender or race of the multi-millionaire. Multi-millionaires and billionaires, regardless of their genders, concentrate wealth and power into the top 1% (one percent). There are higher priorities for social justice and true equality than promoting more "diversity" among multi-millionaires.

It was not entirely the fault of the PC tyrants that I was unable to carry through to become a clergyman. One reason was that I was autistic, which neither I nor anyone else knew until 2007. That, of course, was not the fault of anyone at the seminary. But I do attribute much of my mental illness to PC and its totalitarian, OPPRESSIVE, and dangerously anti-intellectual methods. Because of my failures to succeed in my chosen career, in addition to the emotional problems to which PC greatly contributed, I felt abandoned by God and lost my faith in God's love. This was devastating to me, though I later gained back my robust faith in God a decade later, and now I understand that the negative experiences from 1984 to 1987 happened for a reason according to God's plan. I was suicidal for several weeks, and depressed for nearly 10 years.

I entered college (undergraduate) in the September, 1976. Had things gone as planned, I would have graduated in May, 1980. The problems (that I would later learn were caused chiefly by autism) prevented me from having much success in college. I took much time off from college, then went part-time, then full time in the spring semester of 1984 and graduated in December, 1984. That is when I first encountered PC indoctrination. Then I went to a seminary from 1985 to 1987, where there was insidious PC propaganda, censorship, and intimidation everywhere. The PC intimidation was even more effective at the seminary, as the PC powers-that-be knew that they could easily destroy our potential careers more powerfully than the PC powers at my under-graduate college. I realize now that there was a divine purpose behind things. I needed to be subjected to PC abuse for five semesters, which would have been avoidable if I had graduated in 1980. I needed to be subjected to PC abuse to be qualified to analyze its evil purposes. Had I never been directly subjected to PC abuse, I would not have been at all qualified to write this expose. Again, writing this effort to expose PC as the evil force that it is, and as the counterfeit of social justice and equality that it truly is, has been very stressful and disruptive to my life. It has become an obsession, which had disrupted my prayer life and which, after waking up in the middle of the night, has not allowed me to sleep. I was, at first, fearful of retribution from the PC Elite. Then, realizing that cowards can change the world only for the worse, and that only the courageous can change the world for the better, felt that I must carry on with what I believe is a calling from God to bring this work to completion.

Is there any hope for escape from the tribulation of PC and its tyrannical power? I urge anyone reading this to be very careful, as I do not want anyone to lose their careers or livelihood to be destroyed by promoting the concepts and analyses here documented. I would simply suggest that you refer others to this book, e-book, podcast, video, or website, which ever form this work ends up becoming. The PC enforcers are merciless in their tactics.

We need to apply theology and the Bible in these difficult times. We need to assert the teachings of Ephesians 5:5 (that greed is idolatry and contrary to God's Kingdom), and 1 Timothy 6:6-10 which teaches the highly egalitarian view that we should be content with a sufficiency, that nobody needs to be rich, and that the love of money is the root of all evil. This text does not state that no one should be permitted to have more than a sufficiency. There may even be reasons why some people should be allowed to be rich (but don't ask me to provide a scriptural basis for that, maybe I'm intimidated by culture), but nobody NEEDS to be rich for any reason. If there is a need to fight the "oppressive patriarchy" or to break the "glass ceiling," then the way to do so is not by the idolatry of greed.

There may be some models, though very few, of non-classist or less classist, truly egalitarian societies. Probably the least classist countries in the world, would be Denmark, Norway, Finland, the Netherlands and New Zealand. (Possibly also Sweden, though there seems to be a setback there recently.) There is much gender "equality" in those lands, and likely at least 40% of the wealthiest and most powerful positions there are held by women, but the equality does not end with that.

There is very little poverty in those lands, classism is greatly reduced (in other words, equality is for the benefit of all, not just the upper-class), they rate very high on surveys of the happiest nations in the world despite challenges in some of them, and most people there feel that the government is working in their favor. I once heard a Dane say, "How come Denmark rates as one of the happiest nations on earth? It obviously is not because of our winters." (Maybe its summers as the land of the midnight sun contributes to Danish well-being.) I have heard several times that Danish workers in fast food earn typically $22.00 per hour, which at this time would be a living wage. It is widely disputed the role that socialism plays. It is widely argued by both sides whether these nations are socialist or capitalist or some highly effective combination. I once heard a Danish politician say that Denmark is not socialist, and I suspect that he is an expert about Denmark. I also once heard a Danish capitalist claim that Denmark, after New Zealand, is the best nation in the world for small business. I recently met a woman who lived in the Netherlands for four years. I said to her, "I give the Dutch much credit for how they take care of their poor and their working class." She replied, "There are no poor people there," which she attributed to socialism, a claim that many would dispute.

While I am no expert on any of these cultures, I strongly suspect that much of their success in reducing poverty and classism significantly is their cultural values. They likely define equality in a much broader sense than the USA and most other lands. There has likely been much cultural change in these lands, likely more gradually in most of them but far more recently in New Zealand. New Zealand's history and development parallel those of the USA to a significant degree, not just their British colonial past and heritage, but their status as immigrant nations, where the majority of the population is non-indigenous and their tragic history of mistreatment of the indigenous populations: American "Indians" in the USA and Maori (Polynesians) in New Zealand. Things were not looking so rosy for New Zealand in the late 20th century. I remember reading about the racism there, the violence and crime there, and it looked in the 1990's that by 2020, New Zealand would be a highly disturbed country with severe racial conflict. White, chiefly Anglo-Celtic, New Zealanders were declining rapidly in percentage due to lower birthrates and emigration to Australia, and with the rapidly growing Polynesian population, both indigenous Maori and immigrants from nearby Polynesian islands. Since the Maori owned only a small amount of land, they were highly marginalized. Yet, these dire predictions fortunately did not become reality. New Zealand became one of the happiest nations on earth, the happiest nation outside of Northern Europe, and is said to have the least corrupt government on earth. How did this happy story happen? It was probably because of, not only reduced racism, but reduced classism. There must have been some significant political and cultural change.

We in the USA need some cultural change, especially in our understanding of "equality." We need to extend equality for the benefit of all, not just for members of the upper-class, regardless of gender.

I can imagine many of my readers asking, "Why do you speak so repeatedly about upper-class gender quotas? I've never heard anyone else, PC or otherwise, speak about the need for upper-class gender quotas." It is an excellent question. My response, "Neither have I heard anyone, including PC zealots, ever use the term. And there is a very good reason for that. Using the term "upper-class gender quotas," would expose this PC concept as inadequate, irrelevant to most people, and make this concept as easily detectable as benefiting only the wealthiest. So PC advocates use such innocent-sounding and noble-sounding (but highly misleading terms) as "gender equality, "gender parity," "the full equality of women," "perfect equality," and much of the time just plain "equality," to mislead people into thinking that upper-class gender quotas are relevant to "all" women, and will benefit "all" women, and even all "humankind," while these quotas will do nothing of the sort. They will benefit only the upper-class. And they will benefit the top 1% of "white males" more than 99% of women.

In writing this, I have discovered even more clearly the questionable, authoritarian methods of PC, in just the last five days. I have discovered the highly effective method of propaganda and indoctrination through fallacies, and how their nature as fallacies make them more effective. It has been said that the more people hear a lie the more likely they will believe it. I have applied this insight to fallacies. The more people in a PC-controlled institution (or any other indoctrination camp) are fed the same fallacy incessantly, no matter how vulnerable it is, the more people will succumb to believing it. Persistent repetition has this effect. In an indoctrination camp, persistent propaganda has the effect of convincing people that a fallacy is truth, because after persistent repetition of a fallacy, people are convinced to believe that the truth is whatever the "authorities" say it is, without questioning.

Earlier this morning, I was thinking about why there so few people, well-qualified to document the fallacies and the highly authoritarian methods of PC, have written books or other media to expose PC. If someone can survive years, possibly decades, of being in a PC indoctrination camp, without being convinced of the dangers and the dogmas of PC, there must be dozens at least of such qualified, articulate individuals. Of course, anyone who lives under the totalitarian reign of terror that is PC knows the power of PC intimidation, and PC censorship. It is obviously, as stated earlier, that these people know that their careers and livelihoods will be seriously threatened for any significant criticism or critique of PC. But certainly there must be some retired college professors, retired mainline clergy, and other retired members of other occupations who are no longer under such threats. I think that one big reason is something that I have experienced much in the last five days that I have written this; namely, the oppressive emotional stress and other psychological problems caused by PC intimidation, such as what I have experienced in writing this. Writing this critique of PC has brought into the present, and forced me to relive, the negative psychological effects of PC indoctrination. The negative emotional effects caused by PC has undoubtedly stopped others from attempting similar efforts. I was under duress caused by PC for an aggregate of five semesters in the 1980's, and under a less direct (but still effective) form from 1987-1988. Since mid-1988, I have not been actively involved in any institutions controlled by PC. But does not mean that I have totally escaped the oppressive effects of PC. The dire emotional depression caused to a large extent, but not totally, by PC did not end at that time. I was suicidal for several weeks. It took ten years for me to climb out of my depression. And, until death, I will never be totally free from the negative memories and emotional effects of PC, another example of how PC always, somehow, gets victory. Since I was exposed to PC indoctrination camps for only 2 ½ years, and have been free from them for over 30 years but still not free from their negative effects, how will it be for someone who spent 30 or more years in such camps, who has been released from them for less than five years? In my opinion, Political Correctness should be described as a form of psychological, mental, and emotional ABUSE.

Is there any hope that any courageous soul, or souls, will ever arise to discredit and expose effectively the evil methods and effects of totalitarian PC? What if, by some extremely rare chance, say in mid-2026, PC became totally discredited for its immense fallacies and questionable claims and those who propagated and enforced PC realized that they had been deceived, and became contrite and regretted their actions and understood the true meanings of equality and social justice and social progress, and how PC has prevented such noble values from becoming reality? I would like to dream that these institutions once controlled by PC, would invite me to speak there, and to make my writing required reading. I know that this is extremely unlikely to happen, but I can dream. But even though this is not going to happen, what if the once strong enforcers of PC decides that they would refuse to enforce PC dogmas and fallacies, to expose their truly oppressive nature, and to start producing a true form of progress that would benefit everyone (except, of course, the top 1%)? Unfortunately, it would be "too little and too late." Many years, indeed four decades, of true progress has been lost and true justice and progress will already have been delayed, due to PC and its authoritarian, intimidating tactics.

Do I regard myself as a victim of emotional distress due to PC? I am tempted to, but instead I regard myself as a survivor, and if I did consider myself a victim, I would certainly not be the only one or even the one most victimized. The real victims of PC are truly numerous, indeed the vast majority of the population. The poor and less wealthy of all races and genders, the majority of "white males," who have been demonized by PC, the majority of women, and the majority of blacks and other minorities, probably the vast majority of blacks, whose true needs for sufficiency and dignity have not been met by PC, with its classist, inadequate views masquerading as "equality," with the PC's preferential option for the rich. And, in reality, 99% of the American people are victims. The very deep, bitter divisions and disunity and dangerous polarization, to which PC has greatly contributed with its highly divisive propaganda, have all become a true threat to our national unity and prevented true justice and social welfare. It happened by design, not by chance. The PC Elite knew well of the strategy of "divide and conquer." Nearly all of us, whether "white males" or "women and minorities" are the true victims.

On one hand, I cannot truly find fault with anyone, PC enforcers or otherwise, for failing to realize the need to fight racism by fighting classism at the same time, and that the failure to do so has made the efforts to eliminate racism far less effective. I came to this conclusion only within the last two years. But PC still deserves much of the blame. Had it not been for the authoritarian dogmatic enforcers of PC, their tactics of intimidation and censorship, their suppression of and opposition to intellectual development through their attitude of "We have all the answers and everyone is racist who doesn't agree with us," it is highly likely that someone of influence, with the necessary scholarly credentials and connections, could have come to this conclusion many years ago, and both racism and classism could have been far more effectively reduced. PC makes loud claims, but does not deliver them.

Many years ago, I saw a car with a bumper sticker saying, "My money and my daughter go to [a certain private college]." I later imagined, that if the car was owned by her father, saying, "If the PC indoctrination at her college is anywhere near successful, it will make her totally ungrateful for the huge sacrifice you made to pay for her education, and you'll be fortunate if she doesn't resent you for being her 'patriarchal oppressor.'" I will add that PC brainwashing will likely make her ungrateful and angry, which will make her far less happy, so she too will be a victim of PC.

I feel very strongly that justice requires that each person should be judged or evaluated as an individual, and not by group membership. Whether a person is an "oppressor" or "oppressed" should be determined on the individual level, and even if a true, equitable, and valid judgment is made, someone's status may CHANGE. Take the earlier reference to the Holocaust survivor. It is highly reasonable to judge her as being oppressed for many years. But when she sexually abused her son, she ceased to be oppressed and became an oppressor. Again, all forms of racism, anti-Semitism, misogyny, as well as POLITICAL CORRECTNESS, promote the method of collective guilt, and thereby, promote injustice.

Is there any hope for defeating, or even reducing, the evil results of PC? One source of hope, and I shall ENRAGE PC enforcers by using one of their favorite buzz-words against them. One of the greatest hopes for defeating PC is DIVERSITY, in this case, religious diversity. The great diversity of religions in America was a big obstacle to the total takeover by PC. True, PC had immense success in gaining control of many mainline churches, but, fortunately, the more conservative churches were far more resistant, to varying degrees. If, say, 95% of Americans belonged to or identified with the six largest mainline liberal churches, this would have resulted in a near-total takeover of America's churches. While there are a few signs of creeping PC influence in some conservative and Evangelical churches, even as early as 1994, the takeover has been only limited success. It may be mentioned that currently the United Methodist Church, widely regarded as a mainline church, has been affected by a severe internal conflict between the "progressives" and the

Evangelicals (conservatives), with each side determined to win. This extreme internal conflict has received much attention, and much bitterness on both sides. I once met a United Methodist minister who was conservative, but who felt emotionally drained by this severe conflict. The positive point to make: unlike other mainline churches, where the conservatives have been totally defeated and have essentially been abandoned hope, the conservatives in the United Methodist Church are fighting for their side. Many years ago I was acquainted with a faithful Catholic who knew a minister and seminary professor in a highly liberal mainline Protestant church who personally disagreed with his denomination's support for legalized abortion-on-demand, but knew that he had to keep his feelings to himself.

On August 26, 2023, a truly evil, tragic occurrence happened. In Jacksonville, Florida, a white racist murdered three black victims, then shot himself.(6) This should be universally condemned by all decent people. It shows the evil nature not only of racism, but also of collective guilt, and stereotypical thinking. I am not about to blame PC ideology for this wicked killing, but will assert that this killing demonstrates that political correctness is a failure. Since racism is the result of stereotypical thinking which leads to collective guilt, PC is useless. Unlike the civil rights activists of the 1960's who repudiated stereotypes, PC promotes stereotypes. This shows that PC zealots are not the moral equals of the civil rights activists of the 1960's, nor are they their legitimate successors. PC vehemently promotes the stereotype that "white males" are oppressors, and therefore the collective guilt of "white males." While PC does not intentionally promote the collective guilt of "women and minorities," it does promote the stereotype that these groups are "oppressed." So it promotes stereotypical thinking, which is the first step to racism. In promoting stereotypical thinking, PC removes an effective obstacle to racism, namely, the need to judge people as individuals rather than by group membership along with the repudiation of stereotypes. PC is part of the problem, not part of the solution.

It is necessary to assert the reality that "perfect" or "absolute" equality is impossible and an illusion, and therefore neither PC nor Feminism can result in "perfect or absolute equality," despite their loud claims. There are many reasons why perfect equality is impossible, that have nothing to do with race or gender. Not everyone has an equal IQ, not everyone has equal motivation, not everyone has the financial means to gain access to exclusive upscale colleges, not everyone has the same motives for seeking wealth, not everyone is equal in character, and many other factors. What PC and Feminism have in mind by "perfect or absolute equality" is thus: women must be guaranteed half of all the upscale desirable careers (upper-class gender quotas) and "white males" must be "proportionately" represented at the bottom. This is NOT perfect or absolute equality. It does NOTHING to promote any type of equality among economic classes, or to eliminate poverty. I do not find fault with PC or Feminism for not wanting something that is impossible. However, I do find fault for their totally invalid, loud claims that they represent "absolute, perfect equality" when they want nothing of the sort. What they have in mind is a limited, relative form of equality, one which benefits the wealthiest, and one which many naïve activists claim represents "a victory for all humankind."

It should be clear that only a form of relative equality can exist, and it must be acknowledged that classism and greed, not just racial and gender injustices, are a major obstacle. Not even Denmark, Norway, Finland, and New Zealand have absolute equality, but they likely have more equality than anywhere else on earth. My model of relative equality, the closest to ideal equality possible (if it is possible) is this: make the middle class as large as possible. Provide 96% of the population with a sufficient, adequate, and equitable income; distinguish between needs and mere desires, (1 Timothy 6:6-10) work hard to eliminate greed, stop blaming "white males" collectively (along with other highly divisive propaganda), and actively advocate this model of equality and stop promoting the illusion that PC and Feminism represent "perfect" equality and expose their limitations. I am neither an economist or a politician, so I have no idea of how to implement this. I am only providing this as a model. This concept of equality would benefit nearly everyone (except the wealthiest) and political opportunists (including many PC zealots) who have gained much power from masquerading as the saviors of the "oppressed." If implemented, this would benefit the vast majority of the population (including most minorities), and greatly reduce crime, strife, racism, violence, and other social blights.

We have to acknowledge that we live in a finite, imperfect world and therefore "perfect" equality and justice are not possible, and neither PC nor Feminism can deliver them. As someone affected by autism, I am well aware of this. Take the concept, which I support, of equal individual opportunity. It will not give a person with an IQ of 100 an equal opportunity with a person with an IQ of 130, regardless of race or gender. It means that there should be no discrimination on the basis of race or gender, and certain other factors. It is the best humanly possible while causing the least amount of injustice. However, most Feminists and PC enforcers oppose this concept of equal individual opportunity because it is unlikely to guarantee that women will have half or more of the upscale careers, so they demand preferential treatment for women (affirmative action and quotas) which require discrimination against men, and are therefore unjust, and promote the illusion that they will result in "perfect" equality.

I will quickly assert that I have NO sympathy for any violent extremist hate groups, including white supremacist, Neo-Nazi, racist groups and shall make no efforts to defend them. But we need to examine in depth why people are attracted to them. The overwhelming majority of recruits to these anti-social blights are lower-income "white males" who are unemployed, have limited educations, or have had disadvantaged lives. None of this justifies their actions, but I suspect that PC propaganda plays a part. Not only because of the documented failures of PC to reduce racism effectively and to promote a much more inclusive concept of equality, but also because these lower-income "white males" resent attacks from PC and see themselves as victims of PC and other leftist ideologies. They are tired of being condemned as "oppressors" when they were once disadvantaged. Their response is totally wrong, and, if they were once oppressed by poverty or whatever, when they joined these evil groups, they ceased to be oppressed and became oppressors.

Is there anything good about PC? Not much that I can discern. It promotes the view that equality "for all" can be achieved while gross inequalities of wealth prevail and fails miserably to attack the real evils of classism and greed.

Many people, not just Feminists, would ask, "How could Feminism, an ideology concerned only about women and highly critical of men, be co-opted for the benefit of male members of the elite?" It would be a reasonable question. There are several reasons for this. Since Feminism views everything through the lens of gender, and defines equality, justice, and oppression exclusively in terms of gender with no concern for equality between economic classes and stereotypes women as oppressed, even women who are wealthy and stereotypes men of all economic classes as oppressors, Feminism is far less of a threat to the elite than a more economic class-conscious approach to equality and justice. Additionally, Feminism's rigid dogma that all men, not just the top 1% or so, are oppressors spreads the collective guilt onto all men, without singling out the real offenders. It is not male millionaires who are likely to be disadvantaged by anti-male affirmative action, it is the less wealthy "white males." A far wider understanding of "equality" that would benefit all, including those of low income, would be far more of a threat to the elite than the Feminist definition of equality; the Feminist understanding of equality is highly useful to the elite. The Feminist understanding of "equality" fully allows for the existence of multi-millionaires and billionaires. Feminism allows for the increase of the concentration of income in the top 1%. To Feminists, the interests of upper-class women and upper-class gender quotas are more important to "equality" than the need to provide a sufficient standard of living for all, and to make such a sufficiency high priority. I would certainly not claim that the PC elite invented Feminism. I can clearly remember the emergence of "women's libbers" with their high visibility and vocal demands in 1968. The PC elite did not invent the odious terms "sexism" and "sexist." I clearly remember them from 1969. Sometime between 1980 and 1984, the powerful elitists who would enforce Political Correctness discovered that Feminism could be easily manipulated for their selfish, greedy, power-hungry aims. Between 1969 and early 1984, one typically heard or read the odious terms "sexism" and "sexist" once every three weeks or so; they were dismissed as an occasional though mild annoyance, with little power. That all changed in the second half of 1984. The use of these annoying terms increased fifty-fold in a very short period of time, and would become the most powerful method of censorship, intimidation, and indoctrination in American history. The PC enforcers used the terms "sexism" and "sexist" in five totalitarian ways: 1) by using them to attack free speech, 2) by enforcing their PC speech codes, they were denying the right to dissenters or the right to remain neutral, as the enforcement of PC speech codes forced dissenters and denied those who wished to remain neutral the freedom to do so by requiring all to conform in their speech, 3) by denying and censoring any diversity of viewpoint, 4) by providing the PC zealots an opportunity for nearly full-time surveillance and intimidation by keeping people aware that they were under surveillance at nearly all the time and 5) by forcing students of all races and genders to be subjected to at least four years (and possibly longer) of incessant PC indoctrination in order to enter most high-paying, influential occupations, as well as many middle-income occupations. This was especially effective at the PC seminary that I attended. Not only were people constantly forced to change many words in the prayers, liturgy, and hymns on the daily basis, not only those who were directly involved in modifying these terms but also when we saw the terms changed and replaced with PC terms, we were all made aware. Not to mention that at all times, unless we were in our private dormitory rooms, we were under constant PC intimidation. This also served the power-hungry motives not only of Feminists but of PC enforcers at all levels. If a student at the seminary had said that PC and PC censorship gave the Feminists too much power, the reaction would be that anything that gave the Feminists more power was "prophetic" and promoted "God's Kingdom." When I first encountered PC censorship in my sociology class the second week of class in September, 1984 (that Orwellian year!) when the professor stated, "I will not tolerate any 'sexist language' [in certain term papers, etc.]," I immediately thought, "Totalitarian." Until that time, I never, never detected ANY totalitarian elements in Feminism. I realized later that PC/Feminism were far more totalitarian than I then thought.

One still occasionally hears Feminists complain that women are still being denied "equality," even if women are far more numerous than men on college campuses, even if the majority of professionals under the age of 40 are women, on the grounds that women do not yet have "proportional representation" on the executive boards of Fortune 500 corporations and among multi-millionaires, etc. I shall respond by saying that this fully reflects the unchallenged classism and upper-class priorities of Feminism, and "So what? No one needs to be that wealthy, and upper-class gender quotas benefit the extremely wealthy few, and are essentially not only low priorities but are irrelevant to the large majority of the population." By focusing on the interests of multi-millionaires, the Feminists/PC zealots are NOT focusing on the far more important, true needs of the vast majority, and are asserting that multi-millionaires and gross inequalities of income can co-exist with equality. This serves the interests and greed of the members of the small elite regardless of their race or gender. The Feminists in making such complaints are doing only what the mostly male members of the elite want them to do, without the Feminists' awareness that they are being manipulated. Additionally, since Feminism appears on the face to be concerned only about women and their welfare, this provides an opportunity for the mostly male elite to manipulate Feminism very subtly while hiding the reason for this manipulation and making this much harder to detect.

In recent years, it has become highly common for left-wing extremists to denounce those who do not support their views as "fascists," but in this work I have explained who the real totalitarians are, namely, the PC zealots and their methods, who have been far more successful than any right-wing "fascists" in imposing their views onto our cultural institutions and structures. I have no sympathy for any totalitarian ideology, including Fascism (properly so called), Marxism, Communism, or POLITICAL CORRECTNESS. I see frightening parallels between all FOUR of these ideologies.

One big HOAX about Political Correctness is the assertion that, while many conservative ideologies are "black-and-white-and-no-gray," in contrast to liberal ideologies (including, supposedly, PC), I shall reply that PC is the most absolutist, "black-and-white-and-no-gray" ideology that I have ever had the misfortune to encounter. To the PC enforcers, any dissent or even difference of opinion from PC should be immediately demonized as "racist and sexist." This is one more reason why PC is totalitarian. PC zealots feel intensely that they alone are the arbiters of what is or is not "sexist." Someone may feel that a certain term, concept, etc. is not "sexist," but if a PC enforcer feels otherwise, that settles it! As an autistic "white male," the rigid PC view that "racism and sexism" are the causes of all problems and injustices in America has no credibility to me. According to PC ideology, I won the "birth lottery," and failed to recognize my "privilege," and for failing to do so, I should be demonized. Nearly every day I see several "white males" who are homeless, living in tents, pushing their lifetime possessions in shopping carts, or begging for money. These unfortunate souls should not be condemned for failing to realize their "white male privilege." These phenomena are not only evidence but proof that PC is mistaken in its dogmatic views that "racism and sexism" are the only causes of poverty, along with the PC obsessive dogma that all "white males" are "oppressors" and "privileged." Try telling that to any PC agitator.

Now I am about to become more personal. I sought ordination as a clergyman because I believed, and still do, that the Gospel of Jesus Christ is the greatest hope for people, and that Jesus is the only everlasting hope that the human race has. I sought to spread God's love for people by making them aware of the love that he has for every human being, and hope and pray that some day every human being will know the love that God has for them in Christ. Unfortunately, not long after entering the seminary, I knew that this vision would not likely come true. While I am not conservative on everything, I am conservative in my theology. I believe in the Virgin Birth of Jesus, (though I realize that "progressives" will try to give me a pedantic, dogmatic lecture about how Isaiah 7:14 has nothing to do with a Virgin Birth), his death as Atonement for my sins and the sins of all the world, his Resurrection, and his return to earth (the Second Coming), along with the objective authority of Scripture. Unfortunately, the "progressives" in the mainline churches, to various degrees, either deny these essential doctrines, or dilute their true meanings, or regard them as irrelevant or unimportant. Many, if not most, "progressives" deny the Atonement, or water down its meaning. Rather than believing that Jesus died to make an Atonement for all sin, and that this was God's plan, they claim that Jesus died for political reasons, that he was merely in the wrong place at the wrong time, or that he died chiefly as a social protest. Many "progressives" deny the negative effects of personal sin; they define sin as chiefly present in "social structures" (failing to conclude that it was human, personal sinners who placed sin in those structures), and fail to assert the totally egalitarian doctrine that all human beings are sinners (Romans 3:23), which doctrine does not discriminate against anyone, along with guiding sinners into seeing their need for Jesus as Savior. Failing to guide sinners in their need to acknowledge

Jesus as Savior prevents many from experiencing the true joy of knowing Jesus. To make things worse, these "progressives" promote the view that Feminism and PC are the true meaning of the Gospel, and the only hope for "humankind." This is not at all a message of hope for me at all. Their message seemed to me to be, "The Gospel is for the 'oppressed' only, and 'white males' need not apply."

I must confess that, while at first, I had proper and pure motives for seeking ordination, these became compromised and distorted. With these pure motives dashed, what I sought became a "hireling" position, as I thought that I had no other opportunity for a livelihood any other way. For me, liberal/progressive theology is useless, and even worse, very harmful. It destroyed my faith, led to a severe depression, and nearly suicide. Fortunately, I found a solid faith community many miles away. It later moved to another location much closer to my home, it helped me gain back my faith in God's love, the true meaning of the Gospel, and has been an incalculable blessing to me. It is 25 miles away from my residence, but the difference is worth the distance.

For years I have heard conservatives dismiss many leftist movements as fronts for Marxism, but have failed to see much similarity. Radical Feminism seemed to me to be almost totally different from Marxism. Marxism sees conflict, oppression, and injustice through the lens of economic classes, where Feminism sees them exclusively through the lens of gender (which leads to the absurd implication that male taxicab drivers and male burger flippers are "oppressors," while upper-class women are "oppressed"). Feminism promotes upper-middle-class and upper-class values, whereas Marxism opposes them. But I later realized that, while not apparent and cleverly hidden at first, there are parallels; they both blame a simple cause (capitalism or "sexism"), they both promote a simplistic solution (the elimination of capitalism or "sexism") and both demonize a single group of people, the capitalists or men collectively, along with the idea that eliminating the single cause of oppression will lead to some form of "perfect equality" or utopia. To Karl Marx, the capitalist was the quintessence of evil. To Feminists, men were the quintessence of evil, and to PC, "white males" are the quintessence of evil.

Political Correctness not only attacked free speech through its speech codes, which was sufficient to label it as totalitarian, but through its persistent methods of censorship, unending indoctrination, and intimidation also prevented freedom of THOUGHT. People under PC surveillance, even if they did not share their feelings with others, were under fear of intimidation and censorship, and would inevitably be haunted by fears of charges of "S!E!X!I!S!M!" if they even thought outside the rigid PC party line. This, as I shall assert again, makes Political Correctness a form of psychological, mental, and emotional ABUSE, and even psychological TORTURE.

It has long seemed highly strange to me that while nearly the entire population can easily see and discredit the suggestion that a utopia on earth can be achieved by any means, the "best" and "brightest minds" can be deluded into thinking that a utopia is possible. While many would dismiss utopian thinking as the idiocy of simpletons, many highly educated people, including many of the mainline clergy, feel that a utopia is possible, and by amazingly easy means. Why these thinkers should be considered "intellectuals" is beyond me. I came to realize that Marxism, which long evaded my detection, apparently has far more influence and power than I realized. It can hardly be questioned that Marxism is the largest influence behind utopian thinking and is largely responsible, at least ultimately, for utopian thinking in the current era. I have just documented parallels between Marxism, Feminism, and PC. What is even more perplexing is why so many liberal, "progressive" so-called Christian leaders have been led to utopian thinking. Certainly, Christians of all types are painfully aware that sin is the obstacle to utopia. That includes all types of sin: greed, pride, selfishness, adultery, murder, and others too numerous to list. Unfortunately, "progressive" theologians and mainline leaders failed once again. During the late 1970's, mainline theological thought became highly influenced by "liberation theology," strongly influenced by Marxism, which taught that "social sins," meaning the sin of social structures such as capitalism and Yankee Imperialism, were the chief if not the only causes of sin in the world, and regarded personal sin as inconsequential. "Progressive" theology in the United States, under the influence of PC, would later blame "racism and sexism" as the biggest causes of sin. While I can wholeheartedly agree that racism and misogyny are sinful, (I refuse to use the word "sexism," because that term has no clear meaning, and has been the most powerful weapon of PC to impose intimidation, censorship, or threat to anyone who would challenge PC), they are by no means the only forms of sin. Blaming "racism and sexism" for all of America's problems essentially means not only a failure to blame greed and other sins and social blights, but also means a condoning of them.

There is a need to discuss the historical development of liberal theology, now widely labeled "progressive." These anti-traditional, anti-supernatural theologies originated in the late 19th century, largely due to the influence of anti-supernatural thought, higher criticism of the Bible, and, of course, Marxism. Higher criticism, though I will not go into depth, was largely the view that the Bible should be understood in a non-supernatural, or anti-supernatural, way. It went way beyond dismissing Adam and Eve and the Flood of Noah as "myths." To varying degrees, it rejected the Virgin Birth of Jesus, the divinity of Jesus, the Resurrection and Second Coming of Jesus, the Atonement, along with other essential Christian doctrines (including the universal sinfulness of human nature and the doctrine that all human beings are sinners, in need of salvation.) It also claimed that Jesus never said a majority of the sayings that the four Gospels attributed to him. One of its earliest themes was that the "Kingdom of God" of which Jesus spoke so much had nothing to do with Heaven or eternal life, though liberals were vague about it, but instead meant some sort of earthly utopia produced chiefly by political means. This obviously reflected Marxist influence. The doctrines and themes of liberal theology were around long before PC, but were highly influenced by PC when PC arrived. The mixture of PC with liberal theology made both PC and liberal theology far more toxic then either one would be without this mixture.

For decades, liberals taught that social justice was the true and complete meaning of the Gospel, the Kingdom of God, and possibly salvation. While I acknowledge the need for social justice, I regard it as a supplement to, not a substitute for, the priorities and doctrines of traditional, biblical, orthodox Christianity. Nevertheless, social justice is not salvation; even when properly understood, which rarely happens, it is temporal and temporary, whereas salvation is eternal. While I can acknowledge that there may be a PARTIAL realization of the Kingdom of God on earth, the Kingdom will be fully realized only when Jesus returns to earth, and in Heaven.

Unfortunately, when PC gained control of most mainline churches in the 1980's, the result was an extreme toxicity and distortion of the true meaning of the Gospel. Essentially, nearly everything became corrupted and distorted. The

Gospel was soon reduced to and was equated with PC, its doctrines, methods (including intimidation and censorship), its priorities, and its toxicity. Everything about Christianity was redefined in PC terms and concepts. Essentially, to these leaders, Christianity meant PC and Radical Feminism, along with intimidation and censorship of those who disagreed. Even though I could easily see the fallacies and dangers of what may be called "PC Theology," and could easily identify them as inadequate and just plain false and evil and was never convinced of them, the emotional and psychological toll was immense, as I have described earlier. Though they never convinced me to abandon beliefs in orthodox, biblical doctrines including the Resurrection and the Atonement, the atmosphere in this PC Indoctrination Camp destroyed my faith in a loving God and made me feel highly isolated, though I later recovered, and very robustly. It is not at all accurate to blame PC for all the failures of the liberal, mainline churches. These churches had been influenced by liberal, anti-traditional theology and higher criticism (and, though many of them never realized it) by some limited concepts of Marxism. While these trends were accelerated by PC, these liberalizing trends made them more susceptible to PC infiltration. The more conservative churches, which held to a much higher view of biblical authority, were far more resistant to PC.

It was not until circa 2014 that I had discovered the true meaning of Ephesians 5:5, partly because the Bible that I used incorrectly translated the word for "greed." It questionably translated the term for "greedy person" as "lustful person." I must question the motives of the translators. Ephesians 5:5 not only condemns greed as "idolatry," but also explicitly condemns it as contrary to the Kingdom of God and Christ. Therefore, nobody's greed, regardless of race, gender, nationality or LGBTQ status, can ever promote God's Kingdom. I am convinced that GREED is the biggest cause of social injustice and inequality, not for Marxist reasons but for BIBLICAL reasons, but I certainly do not recommend Marxist methods for reducing greed. And there is biblical reasons for my assertion, as 1 Timothy 6:10 condemns the "love of money" as the root of all evil. I CHALLENGE ALL Christian social justice activists not only to realize this, but to assert it robustly and repeatedly. Yet only once have I heard any Christian social justice activist assert Ephesians 5:5, and that one activist was evangelical in his theology and actively challenged his fellow evangelicals to be more concerned for social justice. I can't say that it has never happened, but I have never heard any progressive/liberal/PC oriented "Christian" social justice activist assert Ephesians 5:5. This is far less likely to happen because asserting the role of greed as a major cause of social justice and inequality contradicts the rigid PC party line that "racism and sexism" are the greatest, if not the only, causes of social injustice and inequality. Not only do the richest, most powerful members of society not welcome such an assertion, but the PC enforcers and Feminists do not want to hear it either. It takes great courage to make this assertion, which most people of all persuasions lack, but that is no excuse for the "progressive" activists in the liberal/progressive churches who love to exalt themselves and each other as "righteous prophets", and who love to compare themselves to the "ancient Hebrew prophets calling for justice." I see no comparison. What I see instead is subservience to the powerful PC cultural elites. Undoubtedly these liberal church activists thought that by blaming "white males" collectively, they were "speaking the truth to power," on the grounds that most of the wealthiest and most powerful people in America were "white males." This is a fallacy, because the overwhelming majority of "white males" were not in any positions of high power or wealth, and that while blaming "racism and sexism" caused by "white males" for all of America's ills, while being silent about greed and classism, they were being manipulated by the elite, and serving interests of the elite.

I am not about to deny that many injustices against women have occurred, and that many still occur in many nations to varying degrees. My maternal grandmother was the assistant manager of a large hotel from 1956 to 1973. She complained twice in my presence, and probably many times otherwise, that she was being paid only half of what a man in the same position would be paid. I shall not question that such was likely to be true at that time in history. She would probably be paid equally if she were in this current time (not 76 cents as Feminist propaganda would claim.)

In the late 1960's, when "women's lib" became highly visible and vocal (it was hard not to be aware of it), my mother became an easy target, which caused immense conflict between her and me. I particularly resented the claims of women's libbers that marriage, family, and child bearing were created by "male chauvinists" to keep women from "reaching their full potential," and "I'm not a baby machine." (Today Feminists would use the expression "patriarchal constructs" to describe their complaints.) I never disagreed with the assertion that marriage and childbearing should be a choice, rather than mandatory, though I resented their anti-family attitude. I learned many years later, eight years after my mother died, how her promising career as a professional ballerina ended. Her colleagues informed her that she would need to provide sexual favors to a powerful man in the industry. It took a while to set in, then one week later it became a frightening obsession that lasted several days. I have absolutely NO SYMPATHY for men who victimize women through such an abuse of power, and feel that such men should be penalized till it hurts. However, I deny that men should be collectively condemned and demonized for such. NO collective guilt, but there should be severe punishment for such men on an individual basis.

I have viewed many videos on YouTube about various topics in Guatemala. One that I viewed recently was about how many women in remote, less accessible areas have been raped. I have NO, NO sympathy for men who commit rape. Rape is extremely vile, evil conduct that should NEVER be excused. However, I deny that men should be collectively condemned and demonized for rape, and the tendency of Feminists to condemn men collectively for rape and other crimes has hampered rather than helped the fight against rape and other forms of sexual mistreatment of women. In Guatemala there have been attempts to deal with the wickedness of rape, but unfortunately the organizations dealing with this depraved wickedness have hardly any male involvement. Obviously, Guatemala need more female lawyers, politicians, and women in effective, powerful positions of leadership. I am also highly disappointed in the failure of Evangelicals in this regard. Guatemala is 35-40% Evangelical, but this does not seem to have much effect on morals.

I have no difficulty agreeing that women should be allowed to be professionals, on an EQUAL opportunity basis (no affirmative action, quotas, or other preferential treatment.) I have benefited from the expertise of several such women. In 1988, I met with a doctor (I don't remember her name or title) who impressed me immensely with her expertise. The neurological exam failed to detect autism, which can easily be attributed to the limited technology of the time. A female graduate student (under supervision) expertly diagnosed me for Asperger's Syndrome, a form of less severe autism, and previously a neurological nurse practitioner (the aunt of my girlfriend) set me on the path I needed by detecting that I had some degree of autism. I have also been favorably impressed by many videos produced by female professionals. That being said, I will once again assert that Feminism of any degree, no matter how moderate or radical, is not in and of itself an adequate paradigm for social justice or equality. It may be useful as an element toward an adequate paradigm, but is not totally sufficient, especially when accompanied by anti-male propaganda and anti-family propaganda, and the stereotypes that men are "oppressors" and women are "oppressed." There needs to be provision for a sufficient income and opportunities for the large majority who need to work, not so much for "fulfillment," but to support themselves and their families economically. And since Feminism views oppression, justice, and equality exclusively in gender terms rather than between economic classes, Feminism by itself is not adequate as a paradigm for social justice and equality.

I am highly critical of "affirmative action" on the grounds that it not only permits and requires discrimination against "white males" (and more recently against Asians and Asian-Americans), but it writes into law and policy the stereotypes that "white males" are oppressors who do not deserve to be protected from discrimination, along with reinforcing the use of stereotypical thinking and collective guilt, which harms not just "white males" but millions of people from other groups. I realize that many Politically Correct enforcers in academia are enraged about the recent Supreme Court ruling against affirmative action, but I welcome this ruling. I feel intensely that a necessary element for social justice and equality is to assert that everyone be judged as an individual and not by group membership, which is utterly contrary to Feminism, Political Correctness, and affirmative action. It is not the fault of "white male" taxicab drivers, truck drivers, waiters, and common laborers that there are not "enough" female multi-millionaires on the board of Fortune 500 corporations and in other powerful positions to satisfy the notoriously CLASSIST Feminists, who are obviously more concerned about the interests of female multi-millionaires than about the true needs of the poor, the working class, and the middle class. These lower-income "white males" should not be punished, penalized, or condemned because not all the upper-class dreams and demands of the Feminists have come true.

I feel that the BIBLE provides an excellent, powerful basis for social justice and equality; not only the Bible must be properly understood but social justice and equality must be properly understood. If we wove together THREE biblical texts, namely Genesis 1:27 (which asserts the equality not only of upscale women but everyone else as well), Ephesians 5:5 which explicitly condemns greed as idolatry and as contrary to the Kingdom of God, and 1 Timothy 6:6-10, which counsels us to be content with a sufficiency (while not denying that some should be allowed to have more), challenges us to distinguish between necessities and mere dreams for wealth, and condemns the love of money as the root of all evil, and incarnated these values into our culture and others, I believe that this effort alone would solve the majority of the world's problems. There would be even more potential if we obeyed Jesus' command to love our neighbors as ourselves, along with some other passages. These passages are biblical AUTHORITY.

I agree with Evangelicals/Conservative/Traditional Christians that eternal salvation and glory are the highest priority for biblical truth, but they are not the only priorities nor the complete meaning of the Bible. 2 Timothy 3:16-17, as Evangelicals often and properly quote, teaches that all scripture is inspired by God and useful for doctrine and correction. "All" scripture, not just the dozen or so favorite proof texts of some highly dogmatic Evangelical or Calvinist sect.

Unfortunately, many "progressive Christians," under the influence of Marx and Voltaire and others (and largely unaware of it), regard eternal salvation as irrelevant and unimportant. Very few would regard eternal salvation as the highest priority, or even as the fifth highest priority.

The pursuit of social justice should be a debating society or a "think tank," and NOT an indoctrination camp. Political Correctness is an indoctrination camp! As such, and for other reasons, Political Correctness is a counterfeit of social justice and as big an obstacle to social justice and true equality as any "capitalists" could ever be.

Over the past year or so, I have met many mentally ill people, recovering drug addicts and alcoholics, and other mostly poor and destitute people, nearly all of them white, and at least half of them are "white males." The "white males" among them do not need to be condemned for all the problems and injustices in our society nor should they feel guilty for their "privilege" as "white males." Many of these people are involved in churches, and many attribute their survival and hope to their faith and God's love for them. Most go to Pentecostal or similar churches, to hear and feel God's love for them. Most of them find their needs met at such churches, rather than at "mainline progressive" churches. They definitely do not go to church to be constantly harangued about "sexism" and the evils of "white privilege" and "male privilege." According to many "progressives" in the mainline churches, these "white males" are oppressors while upscale women are "marginalized." This makes no sense to me, but try questioning this PC narrative in a "progressive" church, (if you dare) and one can expect an angry, bitter response. "The Son of Man has come to seek and save who is lost." (Luke 17:10) This is not to say that low-income "white males" are pure victims either, or that anyone else is. Most of these folk have made bad decisions that have harmed themselves. There are very few pure victims, and very few pure oppressors either, but saying this in a PC precinct, whether secular or "Christian," would make me *persona non grata* (person not welcomed.)

I feel that salvation through faith in Christ unto eternal joy and glory provides a form of EQUALITY available nowhere else. Though autistic, and with other hindrances and sufferings, I have an equal opportunity unto eternal glory, and that this also gives the working class the same opportunity as anyone else. And, unlike earthly concepts of equal opportunity that are limited (an excellent reason not to be deluded by utopian ideologies) but the best possible in this finite world, this form of equality is win-win, not win-lose, because there are an infinite number of opportunities available for eternal salvation. There are only so many upscale careers available, and only so many seats available at exclusive upscale private colleges, which I totally accept, but this does not apply to salvation. I realize that atheists and unbelievers (as well as many "progressive" "Christians") will disagree, but I firmly feel this way. I shall also argue that even atheists do not believe that atheists can be saved, as they by definition repudiate salvation, at least as understood by Christians. Additionally, it is not so much that God "discriminates" against atheists, but rather that atheists discriminate against God. Also, since theological liberals tend to believe that personal justice and justification come through proper (liberal/"progressive") political activism rather than through faith, it follows to them that atheists, who are much more likely that most Christians to promote leftist views, are more just than most Christians.

Some "progressive Christians," though this is far from universal among them, have even defined "salvation" in terms of earthly, worldly liberation from "social sin," meaning of course "sexism," which implies that a woman who is a fire-breathing atheist and wealthy and powerful person is saved, while a faithful, humble, loving Christian waitress or chambermaid is not. This is not just contrary to Scripture, but highly and offensively classist in the extreme. And, of course, it means that "white males" of all classes need not apply. (And, for that matter, most women as well.)

Shortly after turning 40 years of age, I realized the tremendous benefits of FAITH in my life, and that I would have died by that time were it otherwise. I then thought, "How anyone can make it to age 40 as an atheist without giving up hope is beyond me." I realize well that many atheists, other unbelievers, Marxists, secular humanists, and even many "progressive 'Christians'" will dismiss my thoughts with a Marxist analysis that these thoughts are irrational, illogical, and a form of "escapism." I feel otherwise, but I will immediately argue that the utopian and over-optimistic beliefs of many secular ideologues are irrational, illogical, and a form of escapism. It seems highly illogical to believe that a utopia is possible in this world. It is, to me at least, far more logical, credible, and rational to believe that Jesus will provide Heaven in Heaven than to believe that Marxism, Feminism, PC, or any other secular, merely human, ideology can provide Heaven on Earth. I realize that it is frustrating to many, if not most, that perfect equality and justice are simply impossible in a finite world where every human being, regardless of race or gender, is a sinner. I am convinced that a perfect world is impossible in this world by any human effort or ideology. This perfect world is possible ONLY when Jesus returns to Earth to make it a reality. Any other attempt at utopia will only result in dystopia, and immense evil, as the thirty million to sixty million Chinese liquidated during the Cultural Revolution by the Communists of China can easily demonstrate, and as George Orwell persuasively argued in his novel 1984. This, plus the fact that PC began its forceful takeover in 1984, is why I incorporated that year into the title of this work. And human leftist ideologies, even if they did function as promised, cannot make a single person immortal. Only JESUS can do that. The widespread teaching of theological liberals that the "Kingdom of God" preached by Jesus is an earthly utopia brought about by Feminism, PC, Marxism, or any other merely human ideology is a COUNTERFEIT of the true Kingdom of God that Jesus preached. I do NOT believe that when Jesus preached the Kingdom of God, he meant that Feminism, Political Correctness, Marxism, or any other merely human leftist ideology is the only hope for "humankind." "If our hopes in Christ are limited to this life alone, we are the most pitiable of people." (1 Corinthians 15:19) This is NOT a favorite verse of theological "progressives."

Once at my seminary, a professor stated that, because of "modern biblical scholarship," we could not know if Jesus rose from the dead or not, and shared an experience from a student in her class the previous year, stating that he became very upset and disturbed by the same assertion, though she seemed to have no regret about it.

If "Religion is the opiate of the people," as Karl Marx is well known for saying, I shall quickly respond with "Utopianism and unrealistic, irrational, extreme over-optimism is the OPIATE of atheists and other unbelievers."

"Thank you, Jesus, for the hope that you have given me, unavailable anywhere else. Thank you, Jesus, for your salvation which gave me, though autistic, an equal opportunity for eternal glory, available only through faith in you. I pray that every human being will know the love that you have for them. Thank you for shedding your blood on the cross to redeem a wretched, imperfect sinner like me. Thank you for rescuing me, a lost sheep, by bringing me back to faith after a decade of a desert of lost faith." Amen! I call this RECONSTRUCTION.

It is now early 2024, and am now adding more to this work.

I am well aware of the nearly universal threats to the future well-being of humanity, from many fronts: The current war between Israel and the Palestinians, massive poverty and political and economic distress in Guatemala, Venezuela, and elsewhere causing divisive conflict over immigration to the USA, parallel issues affecting the United Kingdom, France, and elsewhere, climate change, and others too numerous and depressing to discuss.

I feel that there are only two possible hopes for humanity at this time. Namely, the Second Coming of Jesus; the other, what I have termed RECONSTRUCTION. I have recently heard from many "Exvangelicals" about "Deconstruction" after toxic experiences with dogmatic Evangelical churches and especially the politically pro-Trump Evangelical/Religious/Christian "Right." While I disagree with many of them, and their tendency to demonize "patriarchy" and historic Christianity, I feel their pain. I feel strongly that BOTH SIDES have failed. I feel VERY STRONGLY that there is a need for a NEW PARADIGM, and what I call "Reconstruction." I have, so to say, "deconstructed" from my old denomination, which capitulated to Politically Correct simplistic analysis and demonization in the mid-1980's, tried two Pentecostal churches (one of them a "Oneness" church which bordered on being a CULT), then a Trinitarian Pentecostal Church, then I found a conservative, "continuing"

Anglican Church (independent from the Episcopal Church and The Anglican Communion) which has been a tremendous blessing to me. I became a deacon in 2015. It helped me to RECONSTRUCT my faith after having lost it in 1988 (which was caused by chiefly by the Politically Correct, largely gay leadership at my seminary and former denomination). I wish to clarify that I am not condemning LGBTQ's collectively. (I deal with and evaluate people as individuals rather than by group membership, unlike Feminists and Politically Correct agitators.) I do, however, feel that the preponderance of LGBTQ's at the seminary and in high levels of leadership enabled the PC takeover. I worked with a very decent gay co-worker for over a decade. Unlike the LGBTQ mafia at the seminary, he never rammed any PC agenda or propaganda down my throat or anyone else's. He is GAY, but NOT QUEER. I even attended a wake service for his partner who committed suicide (supposedly due to a diagnosis for inoperable cancer). My strongly pro-gay mother, were she alive, would be very proud of me. By RECONSTRUCTION, I mean the need for a HOLISTIC approach to Jesus and the Gospel and the New Testament, apart from a cultural bias. I do not mean a hard-core Evangelical/Calvinist extreme emphasis on a handful of carefully-selected doctrines and proof texts, NOR a PC approach which blames "racism and sexism" for all the world's evils. I believe that there needs to be an acknowledgement of the themes of eternal life AND social justice. By social justice, I do NOT mean PC, Feminism and/or Marxism, and I mean social justice as a SUPPLEMENT TO, NOT A SUBSTITUTE FOR, the priorities of historic, traditional Christianity. And I mean a BIBLICAL understanding of social justice, the promotion of which is nearly non-existent, not a PC/Feminist understanding. Once again, one BIBLICAL principle for social justice is Ephesians 5:5 "No greedy person, in effect an idolater, has any share in the Kingdom of Christ and of God." This explicitly teaches that GREED is contrary to the Kingdom of God." Let me say it again, as the "progressives" do not understand it: GREED IS CONTRARY TO THE KINGDOM OF GOD.

GREED IS CONTRARY TO THE KINGDOM OF GOD!

GREED IS CONTRARY TO THE KINGDOM OF GOD!!!!

GREED IS CONTRARY TO THE KINGDOM OF GOD!!!!

Take that, "progressives!!"

Many, many people do not want to hear about the evil nature of GREED. Of course, the fabulously wealthy, such as the Top 1%, do not want to hear it. They are not the only ones. Yet this is an explicit social teaching of the Bible. The PC Obsessive Binary, the PC inadequate view of "equality" as collective "equality" between demographic groups, and other integral dogmas of PC are NOT in the Bible. The stereotype that women are "oppressed," that men are "oppressors" and other PC obsessions, are absent from the Bible.

I have recently coined the term "The Politically Correct Obsessive Binary" to describe the PC OBSESSION with the "white males are oppressors, everyone else is oppressed" DOGMA.

We need to dig DEEP into what the Bible actually teaches about equality, morality, justice, peace, and other topics without any bias. This is contrary to PC theology, which teaches that reading the Bible through the lens of whether one is "oppressed" or an "oppressor" influences one's understanding of Scripture, and if one is "oppressed," such a person's views are therefore more valid.

I feel that the end of our democratic republic, freedoms, and everything positive about the USA is at high risk, and that this will have a dire effect on the whole world. I feel that no matter which party prevails, this will happen. BOTH SIDES are guilty of extreme divisiveness, polarization, authoritarian (even totalitarian) behavior, and pitting groups against each other. It comes with bad grace for the PC Left to blame Donald Trump for all of this; the Left constantly accuses Trump for promoting racism (while providing very little documentation) and other divisive tactics. However, the Republican party does not have any explicit binary, while the PC Left has the explicit PC Obsessive Binary, which is incapable of being anything but divisive. The blame belongs to BOTH sides.

Both the major parties have failed miserably to propagate a vision of a reality of justice for ALL people of all economic strata. The Democrats COULD have promoted policies that would unite the lower income classes and middle class. Instead, they promoted the PC Obsessive Binary, pitted "everyone else" against "white males" and failed to provide economic justice for most of the bottom 70% or so. Had it been otherwise, far fewer lower-income "white males" would have voted for Trump in 2016, and he never would have become President. Contrary to what PC zealots would assert, "racism and sexism" are NOT the only reasons why Trump won.

Circa 1982, I became a supporter of the Christian Right. This started NOT because Jerry Falwell and Marion Pat Robertson corrupted me by promoting "racism and sexism." I never heard either of them ever endorse "racism and sexism." It started when Marion Pat Robertson convinced me that the

American Civil Liberties Union was the archenemy of religious freedom. I increasingly became convinced that the ACLU was a demonic force controlled by anti-Christian atheist bigots. It also dogmatically supported legalized abortion-on-demand and legalized pornography, and appeared to be an anarchistic opposition to fighting crime. The ACLU was ultra-powerful at the time, but fortunately this demonic force has become far less powerful, at least in its anti-religious litigation, since 2017 or so. Thank God for that!

I was only moderate in my support for the Christian Right, but my support for it grew enormously in late 1984 after PC appeared on the scene. I became quickly convinced that PC had become a totalitarian force. The only thing preventing PC from becoming even more of a totalitarian force was the Christian Right. I still feel this way, and I shall explain why. Had the ERA (Equal Rights Amendment) been ratified as a Constitutional Amendment, it would have turned America into an atheistic, bigoted, totalitarian state by 1990. Sound absurd? I do not ask anyone to take this assertion on faith, so I shall be glad to explain my logic. Had the ERA become Law, it would result in the most far-reaching censorship in history. All "sexist" language, all intellectual property and material containing "sexist language" (which would include nearly all literature written before 1984), anything opinion or viewpoint that PC tyrants considered "sexist," which would probably include all opposition to abortion-on-demand, any churches which included "sexist language" in their Bible translations, literature, or liturgies, or anything else that the PC censors considered "sexist" would be banned, censored, or severely punished. If this sounds paranoid, I shall point out two realities: After the ERA failed to be ratified, some FEMINISTS admitted that they were planning to use the ERA to require state discrimination against churches that did not ordain women and which opposed abortion. PLUS, I had never thought that Feminism was in anyway totalitarian (nor was there any reason to believe that it was. Feminism was not totalitarian, till the PC Elite MADE it totalitarian.) In defense, I shall assert that I am qualified to make my case; I went through five semesters of PC indoctrination, censorship, intimidation, and PC speech codes. And, though I cannot prove it, I strongly suspected that the vehement anti-religious atheist BIGOTS of the ACLU would be armed with a very powerful weapon in its satanic opposition to religious freedom. This required very little imagination on my part.

I am very highly critical of the ACLU in regard to its failure to end the enforcement of Politically Correct speech codes on public university campuses. Private institutions are another matter, though they would be influenced by public institutions. The ACLU was an ultra-powerful organization throughout the 1980's, with very little organized opposition, and with vast numbers of supporters in the court system at nearly all levels. Nearly always when an ACLU lawsuit alleged that something the ACLU was "unconstitutional," the ACLU prevailed, regardless of whether the "U" charge was valid or legitimate. Nothing gave the atheistic, amoral bigots of the ACLU any more glee than alleging that something it did not like was "unconstitutional," regardless of how unjust the charge may be, along with threatening anyone they opposed with the "U" word, which the ACLU thought was a magic card or a blank check to mean anything it wanted. This was especially true when anything having to do with religion or opposition to pornography was involved. I felt that, unless someone intervened against the ACLU, the time would soon come when the very tolerance of Christianity, or possibly the view that Christian American citizens would have any constitutional rights would be declared "unconstitutional" at the bidding of the Christ-hating, God-hating ACLU. I feel very strongly that the intense hatred toward Christianity and Christian morality of the ultra-powerful ACLU was a highly significant force for the rise and growth of the Christian/Evangelical Right. When the ACLU said "unconstitutional" it was a code word for "It doesn't matter if it is constitutional or not, or how it would be understood with a historic understanding of the Constitution. It simply means "We don't like it." One thing that was clearly and unquestionably *unconstitutional*, and that was Politically Correct speech codes and censorship in public institutions, especially public colleges. To their credit, a few local ACLU chapters and a few stray voices within the ACLU properly challenged PC speech codes as unconstitutional, but they had very little effect, and whatever effect they hard was local and limited. The ACLU, as the ultra-powerful and self-appointed leading enforcer of the First Amendment and Free Speech, could have very successfully, and in a short period of time, have eliminated PC censorship and PC speech codes, at least on public college campuses. The ACLU, by late 1985 at the latest, could have made PC speech codes and PC censorship a short-lived phenomenon. I am relentlessly critical of the ACLU's failure in this regard. I will never, ever believe that the ACLU is the objective, unbiased, highest defender of "free speech" rights for all. The ACLU showed its true colors in this failure. And, this colossal failure allowed the PC tyrants to retard true social progress for four decades.

I do not believe that the First Amendment gives atheists and anti-Christian bigots the special privilege to censor religious free speech just because such people feel "offended."

These exposures to PC greatly increased my support for the Christian Right, and I give the Christian Right, including Phyllis Schlafly in particular, credit for preventing the atheistic, totalitarian dictatorship from becoming reality. I refuse to apologize for this.

I did vote for Donald Trump in 2016. He was my least favorite of the many Republican nominees for the election, but I voted for him as the lesser of two evils. By 2020, it had become obvious that he had become highly authoritarian, and his millions of his extremist followers, a majority of them Evangelicals, and had become a true threat to democracy. I did not vote for him in 2020, nor did I vote for Joe Biden. Instead, I cast a write-in vote for Ben Carson for President and Nikki Haley for Vice-President. I give Trump credit for moral victories at the Supreme Court reversing *Roe vs. Wade*, protecting religious freedom and weakening the ACLU's satanic war against religious freedom, and (at least beginning to) end Affirmative Action. I have described why I feel strongly that Affirmative Action is immoral, has enforced the evil method of stereotyping and collective guilt, has been a strong enforcement for the PC Obsessive Binary, and has greatly contributed to a political disaster that is now a threat, not only to most Americans, but to all humanity as well. Currently I am considering a write-in vote for Elizabeth Cheney for President in 2024.

I have NO DOUBT that, had the ERA been ratified, the ACLU, the Feminists, and the Politically Correct enforcers, all of whom have an extreme lust for power, would have successfully used the ERA to set up a totalitarian dictatorship. I have little doubt, though, that their current right-wing counterparts will set up their version of a totalitarian dictatorship. BOTH sides have greatly contributed to this unfortunate reality. It is not just the evil powers of "racism and sexism" that have led to this disaster.

Recently my pastor gave our congregation an incomparably excellent sermon about the "Domino Effect" and how Jesus sought to end it. His sermon was about how when one injury or injustice leads to revenge, then revenge, then revenge, indefinitely. It is an important Christian value and virtue not to take revenge. I have identified at least three types of revenge: *individualized revenge, collective revenge, and arbitrary revenge.* Individualized revenge is when one person aims to take revenge at the one individual who caused the offense. Collective revenge is when an injured party or parties takes revenge at an individual OR group who has something in common with the offending party, such as race, religion, gender, nationality. This results in racism, collective guilt, misogyny, anti-Semitism, war, and many other evils. This kind of collective revenge has been done by people and nations and nearly every other entity or parties. It has been enacted by racists, anti-Semites, misogynists, and *Politically Correct enforcers and Radical Feminists as well.* Arbitrary revenge is when someone takes out one's anger on another person (or even an animal) just because he/she/it was in the wrong place at the wrong time, was available, or was as easily angered or vulnerable. One could write volumes about instances of all three of these varieties of revenge. I can easily predict that PC zealots and Feminists (who are so easily predictable) will say that this critique is based on "racism and sexism." That is a paranoid, simplistic response; I will add that to a large extent, racism and "sexism" are caused, or at least exacerbated, by collective revenge. Many misogynists were abused or injured by women; the misogynists sought to take their revenge on women who were in no way responsible for the injustice. Racists and anti-Semites are also taking revenge on people of other races or ethnicities in a similar way. An excellent example of this is when people intimidate Jewish college students in New York to retaliate for Israeli attacks on Palestinians. I realize that it is logical human nature to do so, but that is because human nature is sinful, fallen, and highly imperfect. Jesus challenges us to resist this sinfulness. PC advocates, unlike Jesus, demand collective revenge on "white males" and sometimes all men. This causes the Domino Effect to continue. Do I expect every human being to be as exemplary as Jesus? Not exactly, though, with the help of God's grace, we should all strive to do so.

At the very least, "progressive Christians" who claim to be working for social justice and the "Kingdom of God" should not endorse ideologies, such as Political Correctness and Radical Feminism that contain elements of collective revenge (or any type of revenge.)

Since the early 20th century, a major theme of liberal/progressive theology has been that the Kingdom of God (in Mark and Luke) (called the Kingdom of Heaven in Matthew) has nothing to do with Heaven or an afterlife there (or anywhere else) but refers to some sort of utopia on Earth, and that this is the major meaning of the Gospel. This view is contradicted by several scriptures, but the "progressives" won't let that bother them. Part of this vision is that the widespread practice and adoption of Christian values will bring such a utopia into being. I can agree that a widespread practice can greatly improve the world, and possibly bring about a PARTIAL fulfillment of the Kingdom of God, but this requires individual conversion and devotion and commitment to Christ and feeling of indebtedness to Christ, but I will assert that this commitment is not likely to happen with liberal/progressive theologies, which tend to deny or at least dilute the doctrine of the Atonement.

Since the Gospel of Matthew uses the term "Kingdom of Heaven" instead of "Kingdom of God" in most parallel instances, one could reasonably deduce that both terms refer to Heaven. However, "progressives" insist that it is not so. I also feel that liberal/progressive theology, due to its anti-supernatural bias, seeks to eliminate from scripture anything contrary to this bias.

It is no secret that one of the most difficult teachings and commands of Jesus is to forgive others and not to take revenge. It is highly difficult, indeed painful, for me to do this. I am making more progress, due to my faith that Jesus died to make an atonement for all sins including mine, that sinners may enter into eternal glory; a gift that I in no way deserve. "Progressive" theology cannot provide that motivation.

I am in no way arguing against the need for justice, social justice, and equality in this world, including equality for all, regardless of race, ethnicity, gender, or nationality. I feel that both Political Correctness and Feminism are dismal failures at such. Many "progressives," due not just to political naivete but also due to their anti-supernatural bias, have failed as well. In contrast, I feel that justice and equality, far from making eternal life irrelevant, require an afterlife.

I feel that the greatest form of equality available is eternal life through faith in Jesus Christ. There is equal opportunity for all regardless of race, gender, or other factors. This is what Paul meant in Galatians 3:28, which many "progressive Christians" erroneously claim supports PC Feminism. There are only so many doctors' and lawyers' careers available, and only so many seats available at Harvard and Oxford. It is inevitably a win-lose situation, with limited opportunities available, even if no one was discriminated against for being female or not being white. Salvation, in strong contrast, is available in unlimited numbers. There are many, many obstacles to "absolute equality" which have nothing to do with race or gender. Think about what it would be like if everyone had an IQ of 98-102, none higher or lower. There would be no doctors, engineers, or philosophers. We would have no automobiles, no computers, no advanced technology; the wheelbarrow and the bicycle would be our highest technological accomplishments. Certainly, we all benefit from the expertise and talents of highly gifted people. I have recently read "A Theology for the Social Gospel" by the highly influential Walter Rauschenbusch. While I do not agree with much of what he wrote, the emphasis on the "Kingdom of God" caused me to reflect on what Jesus actually said. It seemed to me that he was stressing God's dealings with human beings (which I will point out is greatly impaired by the anti-supernatural bias in liberal/progressive theology) and that Jesus seemed to stress personal virtues, that is *personal virtues*, and not government force to enforce virtues, justice, or any other concepts. I may be mistaken (partly), but I do not recall any time that Jesus ever emphasized government enforcement of anything, at least not when mentioning the Kingdom of God. Yet, to most varieties of "progressive" theologies, there is a strong stress on government power (as well as power from other institutions such as colleges, big business, and mainline churches) to *enforce* progressive concepts of "justice," such as lawsuits, intimidation to enforce Politically Correct thought and speech codes, affirmative action, and other methods to punish and intimidate those (usually "white males") who fail to conform to PC ideology. There is often a concealed concept of "the end justifies the means." And very frequently, a demand for "justice" is distorted by revenge and greed.

While many have long thought that Jesus was referring exclusively to an afterlife in Heaven when he preached the Kingdom of God, which is highly offensive to theological "progressives," I feel that this Kingdom can and will be completely fulfilled ONLY in Heaven, there may be a partial fulfillment on Earth, and that Jesus' teachings about the Kingdom would call into question the assumption that he was referring exclusively to Heaven. Jesus did say that this Kingdom "is within you," is "within your midst," and will shortly come in power. He could not have meant exclusively Heaven, or the progressive understanding of the Kingdom, as no Marxist/Feminist/Politically Correct "utopia" occurred. I have recently decided to alter my usual plan for daily Bible study to re-read the Synoptic Gospels to analyze in analyze in depth what Jesus actually said about the Kingdom.

It is well known that Jesus taught "Love thy neighbor," and he stated that this fulfilled the meaning of the laws and the prophets. We have all done very poorly at this, especially dogmatic thinkers on both sides. To theological "progressives" it means blaming "racism and sexism" for all the world's problems and making all "white males" feel guilty while exonerating everyone else. To dogmatic Evangelicals, Fundamentalists, and Calvinists it means merely a desire to convert others to their dogmas; including Christians (especially Catholics) who do not conform entirely to Evangelical/Calvinist dogmas.

I read recently on an Exvangelical post that religion decreases the likelihood of suicide for every demographic group, except for LGBTQ's. That reminded me of a Fundamentalist Baptist right-wing extremist with whom I had the unfortunate fate of working for nine years. He thought the NRA (National Rifle Organization) was not effective enough in fighting for the rights of private gun ownership, other extremist attitudes, criticized the Southern Baptist leadership for its apology (in 1995) for its long history of racism,(8) and who constantly attacked [LGBTQ's] (he almost never said the word "gay" but nearly always said "queer" or "queers"), whom he regarded as the most wicked people alive.

Sorry to dogmatic extremists on both ends, but "Love thy neighbor" is not as simple as that.

The biggest failure of the human race is to respect the equality of all human beings in providing the true needs for a sufficiency, regardless of race, gender, nationality, or *economic class*. The continuing distress of the black underclass, bitter issues regarding mass immigration at the Mexican border, tremendous wars, and many other social blights relate to this failure. In dealing with this universal failure, Feminism and Political Correctness is totally useless, counter-productive, and an obstacle. To PC/Feminism, "equality," even "perfect/total/absolute equality" simply means that each demographic group, especially with regard to gender, must be *collectively* represented at all levels of power (or lack of it), wealth (or lack of it), be guaranteed the exact same average per capita income (even though women work an average of 7% fewer hours per week), dwelling in slums, dwelling in mansions, etc. This is an utter failure at equality, though very few realize how to analyze this as such. This means that "white males" must be "proportionately represented" among slum dwellers, the unemployed, the under-insured, the homeless, while those who belong to "oppressed" groups must be "proportionately represented" among Fortune 500 executives, multi-millionaires, billionaires, and anything that promotes the interest of "oppressed" millionaires and billionaires is a true sign of progress. PC/Feminism have long claimed that "white males" of all social classes should be demonized, denounced, and made the victims of discrimination until this is accomplished, and should be accused by loud calls of "racism and sexism" until these PC/Feminist demands are fulfilled, along with passively accepting collective guilt, collective demonization, and discrimination, and being intimidated by accusations of "racism and sexism" unless they passively conform. Now PC agitators are demanding that Asian-Americans deserve the same treatment that PC agitators have long been demanding for "white males." This demonstrates that PC is highly CLASSIST and inadequate, and a counterfeit of social justice and true equality for "all." PC/Feminism has NO concern for promoting equality among economic classes and a sufficiency for all, at least none that I can discern. I also feel that since greed is such an extreme force for evil, injustice, and inequality, no one should of any race or gender be encouraged to emulate greedy, selfish, white male multi-millionaires and billionaires, so it seems highly incongruous that PC/Feminism presents them as the standards to emulate for the "oppressed."

I do not claim to have all the answers, and hope that this work will promote active discussion, uninhibited debates, critical analytical thinking, and a DIVERSITY of viewpoints. (PC agitators absolutely despise this kind of diversity.) Sadly, once again, Political Correctness is an obstacle to progress, even more than greedy capitalists. Sometimes I think that the elite billionaires control both parties, and have carefully conspired to promote divisions for their own selfish interests.

I once logged onto YouTube, and encountered a mainstream news source which mentioned its "diverse" views. I have long ago realized that to PC agitators, "diversity" has nothing to do with a diverse variety of opinions and viewpoints. "Diversity" is merely a front for people of diverse demographics (which means everyone except heterosexual "white males") promoting the same Politically Correct one-sided propaganda.

Yesterday I became a victim of Politically Correct censorship. I had joined an Exvangelical "progressive" group on Facebook. Sometimes I do not know why I joined it. Not surprisingly, many participants in this group had been victimized by Evangelicals and their leaders, and they have many legitimate objections against toxic Evangelical leaders and their ideologies. Very recently I posted, as a response to a post, "Very frequently, the 'oppressed' become the oppressors." I learned last evening that my post had been deleted for violating the group rules for "dehumanizing, hate speech, and bullying." My post made no reference whatever to race, gender, culture, or LGBTQ. I quickly decided to turn this act of censorship into an opportunity to document such censorship. It is debatable that I was in anyway guilty of any hate speech. Obviously, I contradicted the PC obsession with the PC Obsessive Binary, and its dogmatic views that it is possible for someone from an "oppressed" group to become an oppressor. No indication was made by either party of which "oppressed" group was referenced, but I will not deny that I was contradicting PC rigid dogma. This provided me with an opportunity to document not only an instance of PC censorship, but to explain the questionable nature of PC, and to expose PC as an obstacle to true progress of any kind, and to illustrate the black-and-white-and-no-gray character of PC, and its tendency to take revenge and its paranoia. The Exvangelical progressive group provided me with an opportunity. Of course, now that I am retired, I no longer need to conform to PC ideology to maintain a living, nor can PC tyrants threaten to destroy my livelihood, though they have the totalitarian power to destroy the careers and livelihoods of millions of others, and the PC tyrants do not hesitate to use that power. I vehemently reject the rigid PC dogma that all "white males" are oppressors, and that everyone else is oppressed, and I believe that nearly everyone is in-between, and some of both, usually much of both, and I believe that it is possible for someone who is "oppressed" to become an oppressor. These assertions are a bold threat to PC ideology. The ruthless PC enforcers will not hesitate to censor or intimidate or demonize anyone who dares to challenge their rigid dogmas. This vividly illustrates how PC is a counterfeit of social justice, social progress, and true equality. It is beyond high time that people stand up to this tyranny.

It is undeniably accurate to state that the high rate of poverty, especially among Blacks and Native Americans, is an intense social blight that affects nearly all in our country, and which benefits only those who manipulate these issues for selfish political gain. I intensely feel that there is a much greater need for a *comprehensive* understanding of what equality truly means, but PC/Feminism is an utter failure at best and a counter-productive COUNTERFEIT of social justice and equality. PC/Feminism loudly claims to represent "equality," but this assertion is debatable. PC/Feminism understands "equality" to mean a form of limited, relative form of equality between men and women collectively, and to a lesser extent, between minorities and whites collectively, with no regard for equality among economic classes. This questionable definition of equality hurts minorities far more than it hurts "white males" by being silent on classism and greed. If PC advocates promote this is "equality" then they should label this concept as "relative, limited, collective equality," and they most certainly should not call it "equality for all," "total equality," "absolute equality," or "total equality for women." There should be open discussion, debating, and critical free thinking to analyze the strengths, weaknesses, limitations and fallacies of such a concept of "equality." Yet this is highly unlikely to happen in any PC Indoctrination Camp, including one in a setting connected to any "progressive" mainline church. And "progressive" mainline church leaders should acknowledge the shortcomings of the PC understanding of "equality" and its inadequacies, instead of equating PC with the "Kingdom of God" and censoring any challenges to PC.

A few weeks ago, I received an email concerning the legitimate issue of insufficient health coverage for minorities. The opinion referred to the reality, which I shall not dispute, that minorities were "disproportionately affected" by this, and referred to "systemic racism" as the only reason for this unfortunate situation. Reflecting on this over three weeks, I analyzed the subtle meaning of the key terms "disproportionately" and "systemic racism." Of course, racism is not the only reason why millions of people lack adequate, secure health coverage. If it were so, such inadequacies would be non-existent among white people. But, please note, it did not say that racism was the sole reason why many people lack health coverage, or even that it was the sole reason why many minorities lack it. Note the key word "disproportionate." This term is widely used by PC ideologues, and, because of its subtlety, hardly anyone of any persuasion, realize its dangers, or even why this concept is a danger, not just to "white males" but to every other group. Because PC insists that all "white males" are "oppressors" (unless they are gay), and should be collectively stigmatized for that, it follows logically that when "white males" suffer from any social blight, poverty, homelessness, substandard housing, or any other deprivation, that these situations are neither injustices or oppressions, because according to the PC Obsessive Binary, all "white males" are by definition oppressors, and thus cannot be victims of injustice and oppression. And, because of this dogma of "proportion," if a "woman or minority" suffers such deprivations, it is not an injustice as long as racism and/or "sexism" is not the cause. To illustrate the dangers of this, if, say, 20% of the population is uninsured, affected by poverty, substandard housing, etc. then as long as these "oppressed groups" are not "disproportionately" affected, and "white males" are "proportionately" affected, there is no injustice or inequality, because "racism and sexism" are not the causes.

This demonstrates the utter failure of PC ideology. And, I shall allege, one reason why it is a failure is because of its failure to address classism and the greed of the rich as major causes. If there is any legitimate use of the term "disproportionate effect" it should include the indisputable assertion that classism and the greed of the rich elite DISPROPORTIONATELY AFFECT minorities. This shows the failure of PC as a paradigm for social justice and equality. Take that, PC advocates! And whenever PC uses the terms "disproportionately affected," the analysis and proposed remedy is always based on race or gender collectively, with no discernible recognition of economic class.

However, the remedy for PC is NOT to be as far-right as possible. There is an urgent need for an alternative paradigm. I can understand not only PC agitators but many others asking, "I have never heard any advocate of PC ever state that perfect equality means proportionate representation of every race and gender at the bottom, and at the top. How can you document your analysis?" Well, I have never heard any PC/Feminists explicitly say such a statement either. And that is why PC is so effective. It is SUBTLE, which makes it difficult to detect and thus more effective. Much of its rhetoric is implicit, not explicit. If PC ideology made all these implicit concepts explicit, then most "women and minorities" would see the true nature of PC, as well as anyone truly concerned about social justice, poverty, and true equality. The model for PC power was the divide-and-conquer strategy, which to PC was the PC Obsessive Binary. It would have been an ineffective strategy if even half of all "women and minorities" realized its true nature, and that the top 1-5% would be major beneficiaries and the bottom 50%, 70%, or so, had little or nothing to gain. If anything, the bottom 20%, probably far more, or so of all races and genders lost heavily, since PC not only failed to attack classism, but even prevented justice and a sufficiency for the lower classes with its dogmatic view that racism and sexism were the causes of nearly all injustices and failing to assert the role that classism and upper-class greed play. And, I shall assert, many times as many WOMEN would benefit from the concept of equality as this work defines it than would benefit from the Feminist/PC view of upper-class gender quotas.

It took me nearly 40 years to complete this analysis of PC ideology, even though I was suspicious from the start.

I do not understand how anyone who uncritically accepts and rigidly enforces PC should be labeled an "intellectual." No true intellectual could be convinced by the simplistic fallacies of PC, and any true intellectual, even if influenced by PC, would openly tolerate and even encourage, spirited debate, analysis, and discussion of the pros and cons of PC. This shows how PC, not just racism and "sexism," is a dangerous obstacle to social justice and true equality. It also strikes me as not only incongruous and illogical but also peculiar that PC/Feminist ideologues overwhelmingly in their method of determining what group is "oppressed" by comparing not individuals but races and women collectively with "white males" collectively, is setting up "white males," the group that PC/Feminist agitators demonize and loathe the most, as the model to be emulated and imitated. PC/Feminists fail to realize this, as peculiar as it is.

The solution to the failures of PC is NOT to be as "right-wing" as possible. While the "progressive Christians" on the Left and the Evangelicals on the Right differ radically on what "Christian values" mean, they nevertheless parallel each other. Both sides want the government and other influential social institutions not only to conform to and reflect their concepts of "Christian values" but to enforce them. To the "progressives," this means enforcing the values of Political Correctness and Radical Feminism and often the PC Obsessive Binary, while the Evangelicals want enforcement of their opposition to socialism and demands of the LGBTQ's, values of American nationalism, American exceptionalism, etc. Both sides seek government enforcement of their views. Among "progressives" this often is presented under the guise of proclaiming the Kingdom of God. Sorry, progressives, but my studies of Jesus' proclamation of the Kingdom of God show barely any trace of governmental enforcement of his doctrines and values. Much of what Jesus actually taught about the Kingdom of God make it clear that the Kingdom does not mean a utopia brought about by human effort and government enforcement. Both Marxism and PC/Feminism require government enforcement. Most "progressives" insist that the Kingdom has little to nothing to do with a Second Coming of Jesus, Heaven, or a Resurrection. This flatly contradicts Scripture, as Jesus spoke in both Matthew and Luke about presence in the Kingdom of God with Moses and the Prophets, clearly implying a future Resurrection. I sympathetically grant that there may be a partial, that is, partial, fulfillment of the Kingdom before the Second Coming, but this has little to do with politics. When Jesus spoke about this Kingdom, he was referring mostly to personal virtue and faith and how God would use virtue and faith to bless and change the world for the better. Perhaps this is what he meant when he said, "The Kingdom of God is within your midst," or, as many translations put it, "The Kingdom is within you." (Luke 17:21) Much, if not, most of the message of Jesus, especially with regard to the Kingdom, is about personal faith and virtue, which would have a ripple effect on society. It certainly was NOT about government power to force any "values" on others. Unfortunately, most "progressives" would regard this as too "individualistic" and thus irrelevant to "social justice." *The New*

American Bible, in its commentary on Matthew 5, correctly states that the Beatitudes and the Sermon on the Mount, "Though concerned with the relationship between God and the individual, the social implications of the Sermon on the Mount are evident." This is what "progressive Christians" fail to realize in their faulty view that personal faith, personal virtue, personal sin, etc., are "individual" and this irrelevant to "social" justice. This is not to deny that "social structures" play a highly significant role; but sin is in every human being regardless of race, gender, or anything else. I cannot control white supremacists or greedy capitalists. If I could, I would. But I can control myself, and my choices and decisions.

It is worth noting, as many scholars and theological thinkers of all persuasions have felt, that Jesus' most striking conflicts and confrontation were with the Jewish religious leaders of his day for their hypocrisy and failures. This does not mean that he condoned the sins of prostitutes, drunkards, gluttons, greedy selfish people, and adulterers, and other sinners. He generally spoke of such folk in the third person. Jesus never said that prostitutes were innocent because they were the victims of "patriarchy" or "sexism." But many of these sinners responded to the message of John the Baptist and Jesus, while the contemporary religious leaders did not. The prostitutes and others repented, while the religious hypocrites did not but instead exalted themselves. It was not just fornication and adultery that were sinful, but also the hypocrisy, self-righteousness, and lack of humility among religious leaders that were also sinful. Jesus' teachings were mostly about faith and personal virtue. I disagree with thinkers, including many "progressive Christians," that social structures are the major causes and depositories of sins, along with a strongly externalist orientation. *Externalism* means a strong emphasis on blaming social structures, discrimination, etc., as the cause of all or most evils, while *Internalism* means emphasizing personal choice and vices and lack of virtue as causes of most problems; I feel strongly that there is a strong need for a balance between these. I am not claiming that Jesus was a pure or extreme internalist either; as always Jesus was correct. But in Mark 7:21-23 and Matthew 15:19-20, he asserted that wickedness and sin originate in the human heart. Jesus also never said that any sin was justified if the sinner was the victim of "patriarchy" or any other social structure. Jesus proclaimed, "Thus all of you shall perish unless you repent." While I graciously acknowledge that sin exists in "social structures" I also feel that the need for personal faith and virtue is important, and central to the teachings of Jesus. Most "progressives," unfortunately, dismiss the need for "personal" faith and "personal" virtue as "individualistic," which I regard as a dangerous fallacy, because "individual" sins affect other people and society. Jesus and Marx would have agreed that GREED is evil, but they would not agree on much else, and while Marx regarded capitalism as the major cause of greed, Jesus said otherwise (Mark 7 and elsewhere) more than 1400 years before capitalism even existed. Capitalism may enable, facilitate, exacerbate, and accommodate greed, which I will not deny, but it is not the sole or even ultimate cause of greed. Another big danger of extreme externalism is that it is subject to political manipulation. This is illustrated with the PC message that, "You are a victim of the 'patriarchal white males', and we are your only hope." While I do not support an extreme or pure internalism, I feel that a moderate, balanced I feel that a moderate, balanced internalism is far more empowering. It tells people who are oppressed or imagine themselves as such that they have some control over their choices and motivations, besides loyalty to their PC "liberators." I fully grant that one's environment and circumstances have an immense effect on a person, but this does not require an extreme emphasis on externalism; rather it means that those confronted with unfavorable circumstances need even more encouragement and motivation, rather than the PC message that "you are victims of 'white males,' the 'patriarchy,' etc."

I shall re-assert my view that Political Correctness was invented by the PC Elite to enforce their own selfish, classist, and otherwise deplorable vices, and how it has been skillfully used to such an end, while masquerading as an ideology to end "oppression." I must state that, while I am highly critical of PC ideology, I am not in any way imputing evil intent to all advocates of PC. The large majority of PC agitators have little or no motives to enforce evil, but are simply being manipulated by the truly evil elitists at the top. I feel that these Feminist and PC advocates who are not at the top should be grateful to me for exposing this. One real, genuine reason for the failure of PC to promote equality and justice for "all" is because of its extreme emphasis on "racism and sexism" as the greatest causes of evil while being silent on classism and the unbridled, insatiable, and ultra-evil GREED of the Elite. This despicable elite has a vested interest in enforcing its view that "equality and justice" can co-exist with gross concentrations of wealth in the top 1%, and that "equality" can co-exist with multi-millionaires and billionaires, and their intentions in enforcing PC have been highly successful and effective. Why did the news media, controlled by a handful of plutocrats, nearly all of them white male elite multi-millionaires, constantly hound us with the "women earn 76 cents" fallacy? It was not because of any genuine concern for equality and justice for the "oppressed" as many Feminists would naively claim. If these white male plutocrats were so concerned for the "oppressed" as many would naively theorize, why did these white male plutocrats stay in their elite positions? Were they truly concerned for "equality" for the "oppressed" they would have voluntarily resigned their privileged positions so that more women would have these positions,(voluntary affirmative action against themselves), they would have voluntarily organized a reparation fund to donate much of their wealth (what I term "Bracquemont's Challenge"), along with other actions. This analysis, though accurate, does not tell the whole story. These plutocrats in the news media were being manipulated and intimidated by the PC Elite. Manipulation by the plutocratic Elite is possibly the reason for the ACLU's failure to eliminate the UNCONSTITUTIONAL policy of Politically Correct censorship on public university campuses. Apologists for the ACLU loudly brag about the ACLU's defense of the free speech rights of Neo-Nazis in Skokie, Illinois, in 1977 as evidence that it is unbiased in its defense of Free Speech rights for all Americans with no regard to partisanship. But that was 1977, not 1984. I have been unalterably critical of the ACLU's failure to eliminate PC censorship in the mid-1980's, which the ACLU could have accomplished very effectively and in remarkably short time, though I must give credit to the stray individuals and local chapters of the ACLU for their efforts to oppose PC censorship.

At a time when hopeful signs are becoming fewer, I recently encountered an amazing sign of hope and heroism. On YouTube, I viewed a remarkable and pleasant surprise: "Alabama Pastor Declares God Will Avenge Black People for Years of Racism," sponsored by African Diaspora News, and narrated by Emma Ansah. (February 29, 2024.) (9) John Kilpatrick, a pastor in Mobile, Alabama, delivered a sermon denouncing not the "years" but centuries of highly vile slavery and mistreatment of African slaves and their descendants, and that God will avenge the victims. This was a *White Evangelical* pastor, mind you, in the deep South. It took a heroic degree of courage to do this. Two points to notice: He stated that GOD will avenge, not the government. Also, he made no political statements. My response is that he stood in the tradition of the Hebrew Prophets, confronting the audience with God's justice. I shall give two points of feedback: GOD has the right to avenge, punish, revenge, and repay sinners for evil as God sees fit. It is God's prerogative to do so, and God (unlike humans) is always correct in doing so. This makes me recall Romans 12:16-21, "Vengeance is mine says the Lord...Do not overcome evil with evil but overcome evil with good." "Live in peace with all." If God ever saw fit to punish the descendants of slave owners, it is his rightful judgment to do so. I am not urging God to do so, I'm merely arguing that God's judgment is just, and that human beings, regardless of race, gender, LGBTQ, or anything else, are capable of injustice, as can be seen both by the collective revenge by a wide range of people, including racism, anti-Semitism, *and* Political Correctness. Additionally, human revenge is very often corrupted by greed, selfishness, hatred, and other corrupt elements. Amen, Brother Kilpatrick! We need people like you multiplied a thousandfold!

It is my confident belief that at least 10 times as many *women* would benefit from the concepts of equality and social justice as stated here as would benefit from Politically Correct concepts of "equality" and social justice. Political Correctness does not hurt upper-class "white males" (it actually protects their greed and classist views) but greatly hurts lower-income "white males" and their wives and children. Anyone who claims that PC and Radical Feminism are a "victory for all humankind" needs to realize this. "Equality" of groups collectively is an utter failure, and highly classist. We need a comprehensive equality of persons. I shall term this concept as "comprehensive equality." I actually believe in gender equality far more than PC/Feminist agitators . I believe that all women and men are entitled to some sufficient, adequate degree of equality, while Feminists believe that equality is chiefly for the benefit of women at or near the top. I believe in women's equality far more than any PC/Feminists! To illustrate: on events such as "International Women's Day," I feel that women in all walks of life, including full-time mothers, deserve recognition and acknowledgment. Unfortunately, most Feminists would resent such a sentiment, would regard it as a "patriarchal" attempt to keep women out of upscale careers, and would feel that only upscale women deserve recognition and glory.

I realize the constant biblical command to be humble, so I will not imitate Harold Hecuba, the highly conceited Hollywood producer (played by Phil Silvers) who appeared on an episode of *Gilligan's Island* who announced, "You are about to be privileged" as he was about to give a performance. Instead, I wish to give God all the glory. This project was highly formidable. However, God provided the necessary abilities to make this project a reality, and provided me with the highly painful experiences (especially in 1984-1987) that I needed in order to be qualified to perform this task. It is my deep prayer that every human being will know the deep love that God has for every human creature, and how he proved this love in the Person of Jesus. May it be so! Jesus expressed this in his tender message to the Samaritan woman at the well (John 4:4-29).

To sum it up: Political Correctness has been highly successful in its political and cultural aims in gaining control of key institutions, and in manipulating many activists and leaders into believing that it represents equality and justice "for all," but it has been an abject failure in providing equality for all and justice for all. I have no sympathy for any type or form of racism. I dated a Black girl in 1974, I have dated a Korean woman since

1999, and I learned in the 1980's that my pale-colored maternal grandmother was highly likely to have some small amount of Native American ancestry, (which is fine with me; her prominent high cheekbones and heart-shaped face were very beautiful.) Many people think that the surest way to fight racism is to vote straight-ticket Democrat, and that voting otherwise is a sure sign of racism. For approximately 60 years the Democrats have been masquerading as the saviors of minorities, especially Blacks. I am not claiming that the Republicans have done any better, but the continued high rates of poverty and economic despair among minorities shows that the Democrats have not delivered on their promises. Again, this is not due to racism among "white males" or among Republicans, but the failure of BOTH parties to fight classism. The Democrats failed to embrace an anti-classist approach to poverty. Instead, they chose the divide-and-conquer strategy of the PC Obsessive Binary. They, not just the Republicans and the incorrigibly "racist and sexist white males" have failed.

And PC prevented any true progress from happening, partly due to its dogmatic and highly authoritarian methods of indoctrination, censorship, and intimidation.

This is an era of true existential threats to the whole human race. I feel that the only true hope for humanity is the Second Coming of Christ, and besides that, the careful and consistent application of what Jesus and the Apostles, and other scriptural authorities actually taught, not read with a cultural bias. To this extent, nearly all Christian institutions have been a dismal failure. Nearly all of them cite 5% to 20% of what the Bible actually teaches, and add to that little bit vast amounts of cultural, theological, and political bias, added to vast amounts of TOXICITY and authoritarian attitudes and behavior. This is just as true regarding "progressives" as nearly anyone else.

I have recently re-read what Jesus actually said in the three Synoptic Gospels with regard to the Kingdom of God. He spoke mostly about personal virtue and faith, submission to God, how God would bless this virtue and faith, and how this would have a "ripple effect" on society. I read nothing or nearly nothing about how Jesus advocated human governments or any other social institutions to enforce his teachings. Though "progressive" and highly conservative Christians differ greatly about the true nature of Jesus' teachings, they parallel each other in their desire and intent to demand that the government and other social institutions reflect, promote, and ENFORCE these teachings allegedly attributed to Jesus. If anything, the "progressives" are even worse, as many of them equate their own doctrines and values with the Kingdom of God and the complete meaning of the Gospel. Jesus, in stating that his listeners should seek first the Kingdom of God, he made it a personal, conscious choice, not to be forced upon anyone by governmental power. (Matthew 6:33, Luke 12:31). Many "progressives" object to any concept of or emphasis on personal virtue, salvation, piety, etc. on the grounds that anything "individual" is somehow not "social."

Such thinking is highly erroneous and fallacious. I cannot control what the "capitalists," racists, and other evildoers do, but I can control myself. If I could control evil in others, I would be glad to do so. Each "individual's" sin has an impact on others, and on society. This is one reason why I object strongly to the extreme emphasis that "progressives" place on evil and sin in "social structures," and the failure to teach that all humans are sinners (Romans 3:23) (without regard to race or gender; this is a totally egalitarian doctrine) in need of repentance and the cultivation of virtue and faith on the "individual" level. Society is composed of individuals, not just "social structures."

The time is very, very late. While I have skillfully critiqued PC and Radical Feminism as counterfeits of social justice and equality, I feel intensely that the proper response is not to be as "right-wing" as possible or to dismiss social justice as a front for Marxism. There is a need for a different vision, a different paradigm, and an alternative to both left-wing and right-wing concepts. The Left has failed miserably, and the Right has failed as well. The "progressives" in the mainline churches have failed miserably, but the faithful, more theologically correct conservative Christians have failed to produce an adequate alternative. I have attempted valiantly to provide an alternative, biblically-based vision. Humanity is almost universally in an extreme crisis now, and I see the only hope as 1) The Second Coming of Jesus Christ or 2) the realization of a biblically-sound view of equality and social justice and morality. This will require open discussion, encouragement of alternative views (in contrast to dogmatic PC censorship), the atmosphere of a free-wheeling debating society (which is anathema to PC zealots), the minimized use of name-calling (especially the odious PC Feminist terms "sexism" and "sexist"), the elimination of *ad hominem* accusations, and the PC Obsessive Binary. These criteria must be applied, both in secular PC precincts and in "progressive" mainline church settings. I am convinced that PC advocates, due to their failures, are worse obstacles to social justice than the "capitalists" could ever be.

Facts must be acknowledged and asserted to expose fallacies whenever possible. It is a fact that less than 2% of American men are "doctors or lawyers," and it is likely than less than 4% of men have the upscale careers that Feminists find necessary and desirable for "fulfillment." I am in no way denying that women should be allowed individual equal opportunity to enter these careers. This should be incorporated into a model for social justice and equality for all, but insufficient in and of itself. There needs to be made sufficient provision for those who are working for economic need, not just for "fulfillment." It must be asserted that the emphasis on women in upscale careers has limited potential, and that it is inadequate in and of itself to provide equality and justice for "all humankind," and that it is nothing less than a demonstrable fallacy that these careers exist in unlimited numbers, and that "sexism" and the "oppressive patriarchy" are the only reasons why most women do not have such careers, as well as the loud Feminist claim that women should be stereotyped as "oppressed" because most women do not possess them. Most people, regardless of race or gender, will need to find "fulfillment" through other means. And, I would much rather have a godly woman in a position of power and influence than an ungodly, evil "white male" any day.

Before anyone dismisses my belief that there is a powerful, hidden Elite that created and enforce Political Correctness as a conspiracy theory (at least I did not attribute this to the Trilateralists, Bilderbergers, or Freemasons), I will state that the Feminists are paranoid to the nth degree about how there is an "evil, oppressive patriarchy" that controls everything and exists exclusively to "oppress" women.

Capitalists will allege, and correctly so, that a higher standard of living motivates innovation and hard work and entrepreneurship. However, enough is enough! No one needs to earn 100 times a sufficient income, and love of humanity, not just self-aggrandizement, should be a strong motivator. At least capitalists do not loudly claim that their ideology and values represent "equality for all humankind," unlike the false claims of PC. In this respect, PC is even worse than capitalism; the latter does not mislead people into believing that it promotes and guarantees equality, unlike PC.

There is need for both structural and cultural change to work for a comprehensive understanding of equality for the benefit of all (except, of course, the greedy elite).

There is tremendous failure on the part of conservatives and liberals. While I do not applaud most of the LGBTQ agenda, I cannot help detecting moral failure on the part of conservatives. Multitudes of Evangelicals and other conservatives constantly bash LGBTQ's, but have little to nothing to say about heterosexual fornication and adultery. Today I viewed on YouTube a video by a prominent evangelist whom I met many years ago. He correctly asserted that there are SIX statements criticizing homosexual acts as sinful along with 354 criticizing heterosexual immorality. He criticized the view of taking "one sin and blowing it up out of proportion." He confessed his own sinfulness. "Is it sinful not to push LGBTQ?" Cliffe Knechtle, retrieved 5/25/2024.

I shall mention Bernie Sanders; though I strongly differ from him on several issues (especially his strong support for abortion), I will gladly credit him for his courageous and desperately needed denunciation of GREED. On this issue, his stand is both biblical and prophetic. His courage is in strong contrast to the vast majority of high-profile Christian leaders, including "progressives," and especially the "Prosperity" preachers who blatantly contradict biblical teachings about greed and about the directive to be content with a sufficiency. There is a need to LOVE one's neighbor as oneself, and as James 2:15-16 says, "Suppose a brother or sister lacks clothing or food, and you say to them, 'Good luck and good-bye. Keep warm and well-fed,' but do not meet their needs, what good is that?" See also 1 John 11-24, which exhorts an outgoing view of Christian love.

Currently we are in the midst of the controversy surrounding Harrison Butker, who has shown amazing courage in challenging the rigid dogmas of Political Correctness. This has given me much hope in anticipating that the Politically Correct Reign of Terror through censorship and intimidation may be severely challenged and weakened in the near future.

I would also like to mention Tony Attwood, a British psychologist in Australia, one of the world's leading authorities on autism. I have recently viewed some of his videos on YouTube, which have caused me to change my attitude toward autism as a curse. Dr. Attwood sees it as a special ability. Though I have long ceased to feel sorry for myself as a victim of autism, but have seen myself as a survivor, I am now beginning to see it as an advantage. It gives me the ability to see and think "outside the box."

Many times I heard Evangelicals quote 2 Thessalonians 3:10 to oppose the welfare state. "If one will not work, neither should [they] eat." I was disappointed to see in context that Paul and his fellow-workers were applying it only to themselves, not as a doctrine to be imposed on wider society. It is true, though, to assert that in Genesis 1:17-19, God banished Adam and Eve from Eden, and informed them that they would have to work for a living, if they wanted to eat. Thus, the right to a decent standard of living without having to work to maintain such was revoked. There should be provision for those who due to disability, elderly age, lack of employment opportunities, and other variables, cannot work due to such conditions, but no one's rights are being violated who does not have an extravagant, luxurious standard of living. And greed, as an extreme evil, has no redeeming social value regardless of the race, gender, or "intersectionality" of anyone who practices or promotes it.

Anytime anyone who is "oppressed" becomes greedy, she or he ceases to be oppressed and has become an oppressor.

A tremendous, pervasive cause of nearly all social evils is classism, along with GREED, resulting in the nearly universal failure to provide EQUALITY in the form of a just, sufficient, adequate, equitable standard of living for ALL persons. This greatly aggravates crime, wars, international conflicts, massive emigration and immigration (now a significant and burning issue at the border between the United States and Mexico), massive indifference to the welfare of others, etc. Political Correctness and PC Feminism will be utterly useless at fighting these issues relating to classism. Since most advocates of PC and Radical Feminism evaluate everything in COLLECTIVE terms between "women and minorities" and "white males" collectively, with little discernible attacks on gross inequalities among economic classes (except when "women and minorities" are "disproportionately" affected, compared to "white males" collectively), blame "racism and sexism" as the causes of all injustices, problems, and evil without attacking classism and greed, and defining equality collectively in a way that favors the rich above anyone else and protects their interests, I am convinced that PC is a counterfeit of social justice and equality, and having virtually no positive potential for eliminating poverty and other social evils effectively. Anyone truly concerned about social justice and true equality, or for humanity, needs to realize this.

Political Correctness is in serious moral and philosophical error. There are no pure victims or pure oppressors, on either the individual or collective level. Every human being is somewhere in between or some of both.

ENDNOTES

1. Here are figures based on calculations from *The Statistical Abstract of the United States*, 2017.

   There are approx. 759,800 male lawyers in the USA, and 625,347 male physicians and 296,191 male mechanical engineers. These equal 1,681,338 males; in a nation of 116,274,000 men over the age of 19. Thus, only about 1.5% of adult males are in these occupations. Add high-ranking politicians, Fortune 500 executives, and those in other high-paying, powerful, influential careers; and far less than 3% of men have these occupations. Yet Radical Feminism and Political Correctness condemn all men collectively because a majority of those in such careers are men (which will not be the case in the near future), and that women are "under-represented" in these careers (read: a demand for upper-class gender quotas), and promote the gross fallacy that "sexism" is the only reason why most women do not have such occupations. (Based on Table 639)

2. *Journal of Economic Perspectives*: Volume 27, Number 3 (Summer 2013).4

3. Hugh R.K. Barber "(The Pro-life Movement) is an attempt to give women whose work involves the home the same privilege and status as career women." *A Crisis of Conscience*. (Seacaucus NJ: Carol Publishing Co., 1993), p.77.

4. Carrie L. Lukas, *The Politically Incorrect Guide to Women, Sex, and Feminism* (Washington, DC: Regency Publishing, 2006), p. 146.

5. Annabelle Rockwell: I Entered College Happy. I Left Angry (Stories of Us) (8/22/23) Prager U., YouTube

6. 3 Killed in racially-motivated shooting at Jacksonville Dollar General (You-Tube, 8/26/23)

7. Pregnant and Trapped: Guatemala's Child Sex abuse crisis: Unreported World (YouTube, 11/13/2023)

8. *Los Angeles Times*, 6/21/1995 "Southern Baptists vote to issue apology for Past Racism."

9. Alabama Pastor Declares God Will Avenge Black People for Years of Racism. (YouTube) 2/28/2024

www.ingramcontent.com/pod-product-compliance
Lightning Source LLC
Chambersburg PA
CBHW060619080526
44585CB00013B/893